CHUCK CARLSON'S 60-SECOND INVESTOR

OTHER BOOKS BY CHARLES B. CARLSON

Buying Stocks Without a Broker: Commission-Free Investing Through Company Dividend Reinvestment Plans

Free Lunch on Wall Street: Perks, Freebies, and Giveaways for Investors

No-Load Stocks: How to Buy Your First Share and Every Share Directly from the Company—With No Broker's Fee

CHUCK CARLSON'S 60-SECOND INVESTOR

201 TIPS, TOOLS, AND TACTICS
FOR THE TIME-STRAPPED INVESTOR

McGRAW-HILL

New York   San Francisco   Washington, D.C.   Auckland   Bogotá
Caracas   Lisbon   London   Madrid   Mexico City   Milan
Montreal   New Delhi   San Juan   Singapore
Sydney   Tokyo   Toronto

Library of Congress Cataloging-in-Publication Data

Carlson, Charles B.
    Chuck Carlson's 60-second investor / Charles B. Carlson.
      p. cm.
    Includes index
    ISBN 0-07-011892-2
    1. Investments—Handbooks, manuals, etc.   I. Title.
HG4527.C298   1998
332.6—dc21   97-23170
                                       CIP

McGraw-Hill

A Division of The McGraw-Hill Companies

1 2 3 4 5 6 7 8 9   FGR/FGR   9 0 2 1 0 9 8 7

ISBN 0-07-011892-2

The sponsoring editor for this book was Susan Barry, the editing supervisor was Jane Palmieri, the designer was Michael Mendelsohn of MM Design 2000, Inc., and the production supervisor was Tina Cameron. It was set in Fairfield by MM Design 2000, Inc.

Printed and bound by Quebecor/Fairfield.

This publication is designed to provide accurate and authoritative information in regard to the subject matter covered. It is sold with the understanding that the publisher is not engaged in rendering legal, accounting, or other professional service. If legal advice or other expert assistance is required, the services of a competent professional person should be sought.
          —*From a declaration of principles jointly adopted by a committee of the American Bar Association and a committee of publishers.*

McGraw-Hill books are available at special quantity discounts to use as premiums and sales promotions, or for use in corporate training programs. For more information, please write to the Director of Special Sales, McGraw-Hill, 11 West 19th Street, New York, NY 10011. Or contact your local bookstore.

This book is printed on recycled, acid-free paper containing a minimum of 50% recycled, de-inked fiber.

To my friends, Cecilia and Alex

CONTENTS

PREFACE

We all feel guilty because we don't have enough time. We don't have enough time for our families. For friends. For work. For play. And we certainly don't have enough time to learn about investing.

Or do we?

In fact, you can learn about investments and the stock market—if you have roughly 60 seconds. That's all the time you'll need to read each of the tips, tools, and tactics provided in this book.

Despite opinions to the contrary, learning about investments need not be brain surgery. In fact, I think the KISS principle—Keep It Simple, Stupid—fits the stock market and investments perfectly.

Attempts to make investing complicated usually end up in confusion. My firm sees literally thousands of portfolios each year, and the investors who do the best usually follow a few simple investing principles—principles covered in *Chuck Carlson's 60-Second Investor*.

That's not to say that this book is meant to be the end all for individuals who desire information on investments. But for the growing number of new investors who want a "down and dirty" primer on stocks, bonds, mutual funds, and a host of other investments, this book should fit the bill perfectly. Indeed, I think you'll find these pages to be an excellent reference source and an attractive alternative to the many intimidating investment books on the market—books which typically require a weight-lifting belt and a pocket full of money to get out of the bookstore, not to mention a week off to read.

So sit back, set your watch, and invest the next few hours in this book.

I think you'll be glad you did.

Charles B. Carlson

ACKNOWLEDGMENTS

I'd like to thank the entire staff of NorthStar Financial, Inc., especially Avis Beitz, Juliann Kessey, Elberta Miklusak, Lorraine Miller, Carol Slampyak, Misty Szmuc, Jenny Elders, Tanya Habzansky, Diana Jewett, and Amy Sanders, for their help on this project. I would also like to thank the subscribers to our newsletters, whose comments and criticisms through the years played an important role in shaping the contents of this book. Finally, I'd like to thank my editor on this project, Susan Barry, for her patience and assistance.

1

THE POWER OF TIME

What's the most significant success factor in an investment program? Picking the right investments? Having the proper asset allocation? Controlling transaction fees?

While these factors certainly play a part in long-term investment success, the single most influential factor affecting your portfolio is time. If you think about it, time is really the great equalizer among investors. Time doesn't depend on having "inside information" on a company. Time doesn't depend on having the latest computer tools and investment gadgets to pick stocks. Time doesn't depend on having a seat on the New York Stock Exchange and seeing the machinations of the financial markets up close.

Time is available to everyone.

If time is the most influential factor on your portfolio's performance, it follows that the most important thing you can do is to get started in an investment program as soon as possible. Interestingly, I run into many investors—perhaps your children or grandchildren fall into this group—who never get into the game because they believe you need a lot of money to invest or they think the market is "too high." The latter sentiment is especially common given the market's strong performance over the last two years.

The problem is that determining whether the market is "too high" is really a loser's game. For example, how many people refused to invest in 1994 because they thought the market was too high only to see the market skyrocket in 1995 and 1996? The point is that every day you wait to invest, you diminish the value of the one factor that can help your investments the most—time.

This chapter provides a number of examples of just how the power of time can produce huge investment returns and how limiting the power of time (i.e., market timing) can often do more harm than good.

HOW $24 BECOMES $3 TRILLION

If you're not in the investment game, there's never a bad time to start.

Here are a few examples that show the power of time in a portfolio:

- A 22-year-old who starts investing $50 per month will have nearly $319,000 when he or she turns 62 (assuming an average annual market return of 10 percent). If that 22-year-old waits 10 years before beginning an investment program, he or she will have to invest almost triple the amount (or approximately $140 per month) to achieve the same $319,000 result.

- Let's say that you want to fund the retirement program of a newborn grandchild. If you invest $4,000 around the day your grandchild is born—and never touch the investment again nor make another contribution— that $4,000 will grow to nearly $2 million by the time the grandchild turns 65 (assuming a 10 percent annual return).

- Let's look at the sale of Manhattan Island that took place in 1626. (I stole this example from *The 7 Secrets of Financial Success*, written by Jack Root and Douglas Mortensen and published by Irwin Professional Publishing.) In 1626, the Native Americans sold Manhattan Island for $24. Had the $24 been invested and earned an average annual rate of return of just 7.2 percent, that $24 would now be worth more than $3 trillion. (Of course, none of us has a 371-year investment horizon, but you get the point.)

MORAL OF THE STORIES: If you are not in the investment game, there's never a bad time to start.

EARLY BIRD INVESTING

It's better to be early than smart.

It's better to be early than smart in investing. That's the conclusion of a study by Neuberger & Berman Management, a mutual fund firm. Neuberger & Berman calculated the results that would have been achieved by two hypothetical investors in the stock market following different strategies. One investor, Early Bird, invested $20,000 via 10 annual $2,000 purchases from 1967 to 1976. Early Bird's timing was terrible, since he invested his $2,000 every year at the market's high. In other words, his market timing was the absolute worst it could be.

The other investor, Late Bird, put up $40,000 in 20 annual increments of $2,000 each from 1976 to 1995. Late Bird was a much better market timer. Indeed, her annual $2,000 was invested at the market's low point every year—a perfect 20-year timing record.

So which bird had the bigger nest egg at the end of 1995 (using the Standard & Poor's 500 as a yardstick)? Surprisingly, Early Bird's portfolio had a value of approximately $320,000, compared with Late Bird's $270,000.

BOTTOM LINE: *It's hard to overstate the importance of time in an investment program. Even with investing twice as much and having perfect market timing each year for 20 years, Late Bird came out on the short end because of a later start.*

BECOMING A MILLIONAIRE

Invest $4,000 per year, and you'll be a millionaire in 34 years.

If you believe that becoming a millionaire is pie-in-the-sky thinking for the average American, think again. All it takes is discipline, patience, and some lifestyle decisions.

Look at these numbers: An individual who can scrounge up $4,000 a year to invest can become a millionaire in 34 years if he or she earns 10 percent annually on the investment after taxes. On the surface, that may seem difficult. However, the Dow Jones Industrial Average has had an average annual return of nearly 11 percent since the 1920s. And 34 years is not really that long. A 30-year-old who starts tomorrow can be a millionaire before age 65.

The numbers are even more impressive if you can save more and get a higher return. For a married couple to save $10,000 a year is not an easy task, but it is possible if they limit the French restaurants and European vacations. If they earn 10 percent annually, they will have $1 million in 25 years.

Let's say that you can't afford to put away $4,000 but are able to save $1,000 a year. The numbers are still impressive. By investing $1,000 a year at 10 percent annually, you will amass nearly $300,000 in 35 years—not $1 million, but not a puny retirement nest egg either.

MARKET TIMING AND POOR PERFORMANCE

The biggest risk in stock investing is being out of the market at the right time.

With the Dow Jones Industrial Average reaching all-time highs, many investors are no doubt asking themselves, "What do I do now?"

It's only natural that the Dow's latest milestone raises questions in some investors' minds concerning the prudence of heading for the exits. After all, how much higher can the market go?

Of course, nobody knows the answer to that question. However, a 1991 study by two college professors, P. R.

Chandy and William Reichenstein, showed that the biggest risk associated with stock market investing is not being in the market at the wrong time, but being out of the market at the right time. The professors looked at monthly market returns from 1926 through 1987. What they found was that if the 50 best monthly market returns were eliminated, the S&P 500's 62-year return would disappear. In other words, if you had chosen the absolutely wrong 50 months to be out of the market but were invested in the market the remaining 93.3 percent of the time, your return would have been nil.

This study suggests that trying to time the market may expose you to more risk over time than merely riding through the market's ups and downs with a buy-and-hold approach.

 # BUYING AT THE TOP

Even buying at the top can be profitable if you hold on.

If you are like a lot of investors and seem to buy stocks at the absolute worst time, cheer up. If you hold on, you'll probably do well.

A study conducted by T. Rowe Price, the mutual fund giant, provides some interesting insight into the benefits of buy-and-hold investing. The study examined stock purchases at the exact worst time each year from 1969 to 1989. In the study $2,000 was invested each year in the S&P 500 index at its annual peak, and dividends were reinvested.

The study found that even if an individual invested at the market's high point each year, his or her account value at the end of the 20-year period would have been more than four times the cumulative investment during that time. In other words, when buying and holding stocks, even when stocks are purchased at the top, investors usually do rather well over time.

"For those with a long-term investment horizon and the discipline to stay the course, the commitment to invest may be more important than the timing of the investment," said the director of the T. Rowe Price study.

I couldn't agree more.

LONG-TERM INVESTING

Stocks have risen in more than two out of every three years since 1926.

Though the allure of market timing can be strong, the best way to profit in the market is by taking a long-term perspective.

Trying to pick tops and bottoms in the market is akin to shooting skeet blindfolded. You'll miss many more times than you'll hit. If you need further evidence supporting a buy-and-hold strategy, read on:

- Investors who held stocks for five years at a time would have lost money in only seven of the 60-plus rolling five-year periods since 1926, and four of the seven periods encompassed the 1929 market crash. These figures come from Ibbotson Associates, a research firm.

- According to Ibbotson, stocks have risen in more than two out of every three years since 1926.

Obviously, a buy-and-hold strategy does not guarantee profits—no investment strategy does. However, focusing on long-term investing cuts down on costly commission charges that eat away at portfolios.

DOROTHY AND EDWARD

The next time you're ready to throw in the towel, remember Dorothy and Edward Otis.

Here's a story that might help you decide that staying the course with your investments is the best approach. According to an article in *Barron's*, Dorothy and Edward Otis bought 75 shares of Ford Motor when the company went public roughly 40 years ago. "And then we just kept it—that was always my big investment," says Dorothy.

Now a lot has happened in those 40 years, including several bear markets. I'm sure the couple was tempted to sell Ford over the years, not only when the stock had risen and the couple had a nice profit, but also during dry spells for the automaker when profits and the stock were heading south. But the couple decided to stay the course.

So what happened to their $4,837 initial investment? After years of reinvested dividends and stock splits, the equity stake is now worth more than $216,000. Remember Dorothy and Edward Otis the next time the market turns rough and you're tempted to throw in the towel.

DON'T FIXATE ON ECONOMIC REPORTS

Rarely does a single economic report have a lasting effect on the market.

I get a kick out of Wall Street these days and its fixation on those economic reports that are released each month. The tendency is for investors to take a single economic report and extrapolate it into a major trend change.

For example, when job reports that were more robust than expected were posted, investors sold stocks, fearing that strong job growth would lead the Federal Reserve Board to raise interest rates in order to head off inflationary pressures. However, such short-term selling was usually followed by a resumption of the market's upward primary trend.

Rarely does a single economic report have much of an effect on the market's primary trend. More than likely, such reports only provide fodder for short-term traders. Investor reaction to economic reports has been exacerbated over the years by the plethora of financial media that accentuate such daily news events merely to have something to say on a particular day. To focus on the day-to-day news is often a mistake. Investors who chase such news events generally end up selling when they should be buying.

REMEMBER: Investors who do the best over the long term are those who stay invested on the basis of the market's primary trend while ignoring day-to-day price movements.

TRADERS AND OTHER LOSERS

Successful market traders are few and far between.

While it is easy to get caught up in the day-to-day price movements of the market, investors should be aware that what truly matters to long-term portfolio performance is investing on the basis of the market's long-term, or primary, trend.

Granted, there are a handful of investors who are adept at trading stocks on a day-to-day—even minute-to-minute—basis. However, such investors are few and far between. Why? First, being a market trader means incurring high transaction fees, and transaction fees can be quite harmful to a portfolio's performance over time. In addition, trading the market leaves you vulnerable to being out of the market at precisely the time when you should be in the market. Markets tend to move in short bursts, especially to the upside. Furthermore, the long-term trend of the market has historically been up. Any time you are out of the market, you are going against the historical trend.

A better way to handle market volatility is to keep your eyes focused on the market's two- to three-year potential performance. In that way, you won't be spooked out of stocks prematurely. Also, implementing a dollar-cost averaging program—making regular investments in stocks on a monthly or quarterly basis regardless of market conditions—is a time-tested way to build portfolio gains over the long run without falling prey to investor myopia.

BULL OR BEAR? WHO CARES?

Trying to time investments according to whether it's a "bull" or "bear" market is a loser's game.

Is this a bull or bear market? Maybe a more important question is: Does it matter?

I've been thinking a lot lately about how a bear market might affect my investing. I've come to the surprising, and perhaps heretical, conclusion: It just doesn't matter. I'll continue to invest regularly in my current investments. I'll add new stocks to my portfolio. In short, I'll continue doing all the things I've done during this bull market. Why? Because, in my opinion, the biggest risk in investing is not being in the market at the wrong time, but being out of the market when it takes off. Timing investments according to whether it's a bull or bear market is usually a loser's game.

So next time you feel yourself getting caught up in the noise and confusion over whether it's a bull or bear market, keep the following thought in mind: If you're a long-term investor, it may not matter.

KIDS AND THE POWER OF TIME

A 10-year-old who starts setting money aside today will be tomorrow's millionaire.

It's never too early to start an investment program. Whether you're 5 or 50, if you're not in the game, there's never a bad time to start. Since time is so critical to investment success, the more time you have, the better off you are.

A 10-year-old who starts setting aside money today will be tomorrow's millionaire. Look at the numbers: A 10-year-old who sets aside just $10 a month—perhaps money earned from delivering papers or doing chores around the house, or perhaps funds accumulated from birthday or holiday gifts—will see the funds grow (assuming an average annual return of 10 percent) to more than $174,000 by the time he or she reaches age 60. In other words, that total investment of $6,000 over the course of 50 years becomes approximately $174,000. That's what time can do in an investment program. And if the 10-year-old can pony up (with a little help from mom and dad) $50 per month, that investment of $30,000 over a 50-year period will turn into more than $873,000.

A key component in this equation, in addition to time, is the annual return on investment. I assumed a 10 percent average annual return—roughly the long-run average return of the market. In order to achieve that return, junior's money will have to be invested in stocks. Unfortunately, all too often a child's money ends up in a savings account or certificate of deposit—not a bad investment, mind you, but one destined to underperform stocks over the long term.

I think involvement and commitment can be accentuated if children are familiar with the products and services of companies in which they invest. Children may lose interest if their investments are in companies to which they cannot relate. On the other hand, kids will likely have a greater interest in the investments if, say, the next time they buy a can of Coke, they understand that they're an owner of the company.

2
INVESTMENT BASICS

One reason I like *The Wall Street Journal* so much is that the stories are written on the assumption that the reader knows nothing about the subject. Terms are defined, important background information is disclosed, and the obvious is explained. That the *Journal* has nearly 2 million readers attests to its ability to connect with business neophytes and titans of industry alike. Too often, books on investing assume that all readers understand such basic terms as stocks, bonds, and mutual funds. Unfortunately, while I think individuals are now more savvy about investing than ever before, a large population still doesn't know the difference between a stock and a bond, between "going long" and "selling short," between "selling naked puts" and "writing covered calls."

In other words, there's a whole lot of us out there who need the basics.

Fortunately, the world of investing is not rocket science. Now you're never going to hear that from Wall Street institutions, since they benefit by maintaining the "big secret" of investing. However, as is often the case, when everything is stripped down to its essentials, the "secret" is really quite simple. The recipe for investment success merely calls for the following ingredients: a modicum of intelligence, a dash of persistence, and a touch of patience.

At the risk of boring you "experts" holding this book, I want to go over a few quick basics for the newcomers among us who might feel they need to crawl before they walk. My guess is that even you sophisticates will benefit from this brief refresher course.

WHAT IS A STOCK?

Simply put, a share of stock represents ownership in a company.

Let's say you start a company that makes self-cleaning litter boxes. You think it's the greatest idea since the ThighMaster, but your pockets are too thin to build the prototype. You start begging for money from friends and family. Fortunately, you manage to get your good-natured (and overly trusting) Uncle Gus to lend you the necessary $10,000 to get started. In return for the $10,000, you agree to give Uncle Gus 20 percent of your new company. Uncle Gus' ownership is in the form of stock. Uncle Gus receives stock certificates showing his 20 percent ownership in No Hands Litter Removal, Inc. (NHLR).

One characteristic of stock is that it can be bought and sold.

Let's say that Uncle Gus has had a few bad days at the track and is now on the hook for $8,000 to his bookie. Uncle Gus doesn't have $8,000 in cash. But he still has that 20 percent ownership in your litter-removal company. Uncle Gus can sell the stock to help raise the money he needs to keep away the knee breakers. He manages to talk your Aunt Erma into buying the 20 percent stake for $8,000.

As you can see from this sale, the laws of supply and demand ultimately determine a stock's price. (This is a concept that is often lost even on the most sophisticated investors.) Uncle Gus needed the money and was willing to take a $2,000 loss to sell the stock. But even though Aunt Erma paid less than Uncle Gus for the stock, Aunt Erma still owns 20 percent of the company. What is also important to understand is that stocks do not necessarily have to trade on any stock exchange in order to be bought and sold.

WHAT DOES "GOING PUBLIC" MEAN?

Going public means that shares in your company are sold via an initial public offering.

Now, let's say your litter-removal system draws the attention of a buyer at Wal-Mart Stores, and the buyer wants to purchase 20,000 units. Unfortunately, you've gone through the $10,000 your Uncle Gus gave you, and your Aunt Erma's cash flow is next to nothing. You need money. What can you do?

Enter your old college roommate, Dex Dexter. When Dex graduated, he went to work on Wall Street for an investment banking firm. One business of an investment bank is to "take companies public." What that means is that the investment bank arranges a mass sale of the company's stock to hundreds and even thousands of investors in order to raise money for the company. Dex talks to you about taking No Hands Litter Removal, Inc.

public. Since you need the money, you agree. Dex's firm performs an initial public offering by offering NHLR to individual investors at a price Dex's firm sets at $2 per share.

The offering is a success, and Dex's firm manages to sell 1 million shares of NHLR at $2 per share to individual investors and mutual funds throughout the country. The deal brings in $2 million. Dex's firm takes its underwriting fee of $200,000, leaving you with $1.8 million to start building the units for Wal-Mart.

Of course, now that you have stockholders in your company, you have new owners. The terms of the initial public offering stated that outside investors would own 80 percent of the company following the offering. That means you own only 16 percent of the company, and Aunt Erma's ownership is now 4 percent. (You can find these numbers if you remember that you initially owned 80 percent, so you now own 80 percent of the remaining 20 percent, or 16 percent; Aunt Erma owns 20 percent of the remaining 20 percent, or 4 percent.)

When a company goes public, its shares begin trading on one of three stock exchanges—the New York Stock Exchange, the American Stock Exchange, or the Nasdaq stock exchange. The Nasdaq is home to most small new companies, so that's where your shares trade. The Nasdaq exchange assigns a stock symbol to your shares—NHLR. The exchange's main job is to facilitate a liquid trading market for your stock and all other stocks listed on the exchange.

One other lesson to be learned from our little story is

this: Starting a company that eventually goes public can make you and your early investors rich. I'm sure many of you are feeling sorry for Aunt Erma now that she owns only 4 percent of the company when she previously owned 20 percent. Don't weep for Erma. Aunt Erma now owns 4 percent of a company valued at $2.5 million. (Remember: The 80 percent owned by outsiders is worth $2 million, which puts a value on the entire company of $2.5 million.) That's $100,000.

Not bad for an $8,000 investment. And your 16 percent ownership is worth $400,000.

Now you know why everyone wants to be the next Bill Gates.

WHAT IS A BOND?

A bond is a debt instrument issued by a company.

Let's imagine that your litter-removal system becomes a big hit. Wal-Mart sells out of its initial 20,000-unit purchase and wants 50,000 more units. That's the good news. The bad news is that, while you made nice profits on the initial sale to Wal-Mart, you don't have enough money from retained profits and cash flow to build the 50,000 units.

You need more money.

What are your options? You could sell more shares of stock to the public through another stock offering. However, every new share you issue dilutes your ownership, as well as the ownership of other investors.

Alternatively, you can issue bonds.

A bond is a debt instrument issued by a company. An investor who purchases the company's bond becomes a creditor of the company. In effect, the bondholder loans the company money. In return, the bondholder is paid interest and is promised the return of his or her money at the end of some period of time.

You talk to your good friend Dex Dexter, whose firm underwrites the issuance of $2 million worth of bonds. The bonds have a maturity of 10 years. In other words, at the end of 10 years, the bonds are redeemed by the company, and the company must pay the bondholder what is called "par" for each bond. Bonds usually have a par value of $1,000 at the end of maturity. Each bond also carries a coupon rate of 10 percent. This is the interest paid on the bonds to bondholders. If the bonds are sold for $1,000 apiece, each bondholder will receive $100 a year in interest (10 percent of $1,000) for each bond held.

Dex's firm goes through the bond underwriting and sells $2 million worth of bonds. On the plus side, you still own 16 percent of the company. Furthermore, your company can deduct the interest payments it makes to bondholders from taxable income. However, you are now on the pan for $200,000 per year to bondholders in the form of interest. Furthermore, if your firm goes bankrupt, the bondholders, since they are creditors, are higher on the food chain than common stockholders should you have to liquidate assets.

This is an important point to remember: A bondholder has no ownership in the company. However, in the event of a bankruptcy, bondholders receive any money before funds flow to the common stockholders.

BONDS AND INTEREST RATES

Rising interest rates are bad for bond prices.

An important relationship for a bond investor to understand is the interplay between bonds and interest rates. In a nutshell, rising interest rates are bad for bonds; falling interest rates are good.

Here's why. Say you buy a 10-year bond for $1,000. The bond pays a coupon rate of 7 percent. Now, let's say interest rates begin to rise to the point that investors require an 8 percent return to buy your 10-year bond. Since the coupon rate is fixed at 7 percent ($70 interest per bond), the value of your bond must drop to $875 for the yield to equal 8 percent.

Conversely, if interest rates decline and investors are willing to accept 6 percent for your 10-year bond, the bond value would rise to $1,166 per bond ($70 in coupons divided by $1,166 is 6 percent).

Two more relationships between bonds and interest rates are important to understand. First, the greater the maturity of the bond (the more years until the bond comes due), the greater effect interest rates will have on the bond value. A 30-year bond will be more adversely affected by rising interest rates (or more favorably affected by falling rates) than a 5-year bond. Second, lower coupon rate bonds will be more adversely affected by rising interest rates than higher coupon rate bonds. For example, when interest rates rise, a bond that pays a coupon rate of 3 percent will fall more dramatically than a bond that pays a coupon rate of 10 percent.

WHAT DOES IT MEAN WHEN A BOND IS "CALLED"?

If a bond yield seems too good to be true, the bond may soon be called.

When most bonds are issued, they carry "call" provisions. A call provision gives the company the right to redeem a bond from shareholders. When a bond is called, the shareholder must return the bond to the company. The call provision will carry the price at which a company must redeem the bond from shareholders.

A call provision is an insurance policy for a company in the event of a dramatic drop in interest rates. For example, a company issues bonds with a 30-year maturity and a 12 percent annual coupon rate. Five years go by, and suddenly interest rates plummet dramatically to the point where 30-year bonds are being issued with a 7 percent coupon rate. A company paying 12 percent per year on 30-year bonds is not going to look too kindly on paying such a high rate if similar bonds are now yielding 5 percentage points lower.

If a company has a call provision, it may decide to buy back the high-yielding bonds from shareholders with proceeds obtained by selling lower-yielding bonds. By swapping lower-yielding bonds for higher-yielding bonds, a company dramatically reduces its annual interest payments.

Before buying any bond, make sure you understand the call provisions. I've seen investors buy high-yielding bonds only to see the bonds called away from them after a few months. In fact, if you see a bond yield that seems too good to be true, it usually means one of two things:

- The company's financial situation is toast and there's a threat that the bond issuer will default on bond payments.

- The bond is a likely candidate to be called.

WHAT IS A JUNK BOND?

Junk bonds are issued by companies with less-than-stellar financial positions.

One investment vehicle that has run in and out of favor over the years is the junk bond. The use of the word "junk" refers to the issuing company's less-than-stellar financial position. Junk bonds are those rated BB or lower by Standard & Poor's rating agency or BA or lower by Moody's, another rating agency.

Because of the tenuous financial position of the issuing company—and the relative riskiness of the bonds defaulting—junk bonds generally carry higher coupon rates to compensate investors for assuming the higher level of risk.

One way to lower your risk of investing in junk bonds is to invest in a mutual fund that invests in a number of junk bonds. One junk bond fund that I like is the Fidelity Capital & Income Fund (800-544-8888).

Keep in mind that investing in junk bonds entails other risks in addition to default. Interest rates will affect the value of bonds. Higher interest rates mean lower junk bond prices, and vice versa. If you invest in junk bonds or junk bond funds, it's best to limit your exposure to no more than 10 percent to 15 percent of your entire portfolio.

WHAT IS A CONVERTIBLE BOND?

Think of a convertible bond as a cross between a stock and a bond.

A convertible bond is a form of debt instrument issued by a company. It can be thought of as a hybrid between a stock and a bond. A convertible is issued in the same way as a regular bond—with a certain maturity and coupon rate. However, an added feature is the ability to "convert" the bond into common stock at some conversion ratio.

For example, a company issues a convertible bond that matures in 15 years and pays interest of 5 percent per year. What makes this a convertible bond is that bondholders have the option of converting into common stock at the rate of 36.25 shares of stock for every bond. The conversion capability gives the bondholder options going forward, especially if the underlying stock does extremely well and creates a situation when it would be advantageous to convert to the common stock.

Why does a company issue convertible bonds? One reason is that the interest paid on convertibles is usually lower than interest paid on bonds without conversion capability. Convertible bondholders are still creditors of the company and are not owners until they convert their holdings to common stock. Convertible bondholders are usually subordinate to regular bondholders in the case of bankruptcy but are paid before any funds flow to common shareholders.

WHAT IS A ZERO-COUPON BOND?

Zero-coupon bonds are popular instruments for funding future liabilities.

A zero-coupon bond is exactly what the name implies—a bond with no annual coupon rate. In other words, zero-coupon bonds don't pay annual interest to shareholders. Unlike traditional bonds, which are issued at par (usually $1,000), zero-coupon bonds are issued at deep discounts to par and pay par at maturity.

For example, a 10-year zero-coupon bond with a face value of $1,000 may cost $500 to purchase (the price depends on prevailing interest rates and the creditworthiness of the issuer). Investors who pay $500 are assured (as long as the bond issuer does not default) that they will receive $1,000 at the time of maturity 10 years hence.

Zero-coupon bonds are popular investments for individuals who are funding certain long-term liabilities. Let's say you face college tuition payments beginning 10 years from now and continuing for 4 years. You might buy zero-coupon bonds today that come due to meet your tuition liabilities 10, 11, 12, and 13 years from now.

Another attraction of zero-coupon bonds is that holders avoid "reinvestment risk." Reinvestment risk is the possibility that interest payments received from traditional bonds will have to be reinvested at lower rates. With zero-coupon bonds, there are no coupon payments and, therefore, no reinvestment risk.

Investors in zero-coupon bonds need to understand two important points:

- Even though no interest is paid by the company on the bonds, holders of zero-coupon bonds will be taxed each year on the "implicit" interest that accrues. Thus, you might want to consider holding zero-coupon bonds in tax-deferred portfolios, such as an Individual

Retirement Account. You could also consider investing in a tax-exempt zero-coupon bond issued by a municipality.

- Low-coupon bonds react more violently to interest rates than high-coupon bonds. A zero-coupon bond will be greatly affected by interest-rate movements. The fact that the bond will fluctuate in value sharply depending on interest-rate movements will not affect the bond's value at the time of maturity. It will affect the value in the years leading up to maturity. Therefore, if you find yourself needing money and you liquidate a zero-coupon bond prior to maturity, you could face a big surprise if interest rates have risen.

100-YEAR BONDS

Remember that default risk increases with bond maturities.

I've heard of long-term investing, but this seems a bit ridiculous. Walt Disney issued bonds in 1993 that mature in the year 2093. The sale by Disney of the 100-year bonds was the first issuance of century-long debt in nearly four decades. Following the Disney offering, Coca-Cola offered its own 100-year bonds.

What both companies did by issuing debt that matures so far out was to lock up low interest rates for a very long term. In the case of Coca-Cola's debt, the bonds were priced to yield 7.45 percent, just slightly above the yield on 30-year Treasury bonds. Quite frankly, the sale was a giant coup for the firms given the low rates on the bonds.

From the investor's standpoint, the same can't be said, in my opinion. Given the long-term nature of the bonds, their prices will fluctuate dramatically with interest-rate movements. Furthermore, default risk is increased given the long maturity period.

Disney and Coca-Cola are exceptional companies. Still, trying to anticipate how each will be doing 100 years from now is next to impossible. If other companies take the lead of Coca-Cola and Disney and issue 100-year bonds, I suggest you take a pass.

WHAT IS A MUTUAL FUND?

Mutual funds provide a way for investors with limited funds to own a diversified basket of stocks.

You'd have to be an outerspace alien not to have at least heard the term "mutual fund." It's surprising, however, the number of people who don't know what these investments are or how they work. In fact, many individuals who own mutual funds via their company's pension plan or 401(k) have no clue what "net asset value" or "no load" means.

Mutual funds are investment companies which take in funds from many individuals, commingle the money, and buy a portfolio of stocks that they manage.

Popular fund families include Vanguard, Fidelity, and T. Rowe Price. The fund company usually assigns a fund manager to the particular portfolio. In many cases, this fund manager is so young as to have no recollection of the Nixon years.

Mutual funds provide a way for investors with limited dollars—many mutual funds have minimum investments of $1,000 or less—to have portfolio diversification as well as professional money management.

Investors can purchase mutual funds through a broker or directly with the fund family. "No-load" funds are sold to investors without an upfront sales fee. To join most no-load funds, you call the fund family directly via a toll-free number, and the fund group sends you the necessary enrollment information and fund prospectus. The prospectus explains the details of the funds—fees, management styles, and so on. "Load" funds carry a sales fee—which may range from as little as 1 percent of your investment to 5 percent or more of your investment—and are usually sold by brokers. Mutual funds also have annual management fees. These are the fees paid to the investment company for managing the portfolio. These fees can vary dramatically, from as low as 0.25 percent of your fund's assets to 2 percent or more a year.

Investors buy and sell shares in the fund at the "net asset value." This is the total of the fund's assets minus any liabilities. Most mutual funds list their net asset values daily in *The Wall Street Journal*.

An excellent source for ongoing coverage of mutual

funds is *Morningstar Mutual Funds*. The guide is found in most libraries or by calling (800) 735-0700.

WHAT IS A PREFERRED STOCK?

Preferred stocks are primarily income vehicles.

C ompanies can issue two kinds of stock: common stock and preferred stock.

Preferred stock has preferred status over common shares. Preferred stockholders receive their dividend payments after interest is paid on bonds and before dividends are paid on common stock.

Most preferred stocks are cumulative preferred shares. This means that if a dividend payment is skipped because of the company's poor performance, it will be paid later when earnings recover and before any dividends are paid on the common shares. Preferreds are issued with a fixed coupon rate. Just as interest rates affect bond performance, so interest-rate fluctuations affect the value of preferred stocks.

Preferred stocks are primarily income investments. Appreciation prospects for preferred stocks, relative to common stock, are limited. The fixed nature of the dividend is also different from the flexible dividend policy of common shares. Since preferred dividends do not adjust upward over time, the ability of preferreds to keep pace with inflation is limited.

I'm not a huge fan of preferreds, except as vehicles to boost your annual income stream. A good place to start is with preferreds issued by high-quality electric utilities. In this group, I particularly like Duke Power. You can also invest in preferred stocks via a mutual fund. The Vanguard Preferred Stock Fund (800-662-7447) offers an attractive way to diversify investments in preferred stocks.

INVESTING OVERSEAS WITH ADRs

The easiest way to invest in individual foreign companies is via American Depositary Receipts.

It's becoming easier to invest in overseas companies. The easiest way to diversify among international stocks is via an international mutual fund. However, it's possible to buy individual stocks as well via American Depositary Receipts (ADRs).

ADRs are issued by U.S. banks against the actual shares of foreign companies held in trust by a branch or correspondent institution overseas. ADRs have become popular in recent years as a way to invest abroad, and it's likely that this popularity will grow as the number of ADRs increases. Often, ADRs aren't issued on a share-for-share basis. Instead, one ADR may be the equivalent of 5 or 10 ordinary shares of the company.

To be sure, investing overseas has its pitfalls. First, the country's currency value relative to the U.S. dollar can affect returns. Second, political instability can have an impact on foreign investments. However, for investors wanting to build a diversified portfolio, investing overseas, through either ADRs or mutual funds, is an excellent strategy.

WHAT IS A DIVIDEND?

Dividends are paid out of a company's earnings stream.

A company's dividend is the amount of money that the firm pays to shareholders for owning its stock.

Dividends are usually paid every three months. Since companies pay dividends out of profits, a company must make a decision on how much in profits to keep and how much to distribute to shareholders. Small, fast-growing companies usually want to retain profits to fund growth. Larger companies, whose growth prospects are more limited, often choose to return a greater portion of earnings to shareholders in the form of dividends.

Just because a company does not pay a dividend does not make it a bad investment. Microsoft, the software giant, has never paid a dividend, yet it has been an extremely profitable investment for shareholders. Microsoft chooses to retain its earnings to fund growth.

Companies are not obligated to pay dividends on stock. In fact, it is not uncommon for a company to cut or even eliminate dividend payments if business is poor. Conversely, some companies increase dividends at least once a year. Dividend increases often represent a positive signal by the corporation that the firm is confident of its future. Stock prices usually react favorably to dividend increases.

Investors should note that dividends are considered ordinary income for tax purposes. You have to account for dividend income at tax time. Companies or your broker will send you a 1099 form showing the amount of dividends you received during the year.

WHAT IS THE "EX-DIVIDEND" DATE?

The date that truly matters to dividend-seeking investors is not the dividend record date, but the "ex-dividend" date.

Tell me if this sounds familiar.

You buy a stock a day before the "record date" for the dividend payment, thinking you are entitled to receive the dividend. When the dividend check doesn't arrive, you call the broker, who informs you that you aren't entitled to the dividend. "What gives?" you say to the broker. He replies that you didn't buy the stock prior to the ex-dividend date. At this point, you hang up the phone and call your attorney, because you think the broker is ripping you off.

The broker isn't.

When companies declare a dividend, they usually designate a record date. Shareholders of record on the record date are entitled to receive the dividend. Unfortunately, if you buy the stock a day or two before the record date, you aren't entitled to receive the dividend.

When you buy stock through your broker, your stock trade is settled in three days. In order to be a stockholder of record for a dividend, your stock trade has to be settled on or prior to the record date, which means you need to buy the stock through the broker at least three days prior to the record date. This is the ex-dividend date.

A simple example should clear up this often confusing situation. Say a company has stated that it will pay a dividend to all shareholders of record on Friday, September 28. Keep in mind that a stock trade takes three business days to settle. Thus, the ex-dividend date is Wednesday (the record date counts as one day). That date is important, since investors who make a buy transaction through their brokers on or after Wednesday will not receive the dividend.

When a stock goes ex-dividend, it is denoted by an X in the stock-quote pages next to the stock. If you buy a stock after it goes ex-dividend, you will not receive the dividend. However, don't feel that you're being cheated by not receiving the dividend. A stock's price drops by the quarterly dividend amount when it goes ex-dividend; investors who buy after a stock goes ex-dividend are buying the stock at a lower price than investors who bought prior to the ex-dividend date and are entitled to the dividend.

REMEMBER: *The date that truly matters to dividend-seeking investors is not the record date, but the ex-dividend date. To find the ex-dividend date, start with the record date, and count back three business days. For example, if the record date falls on a Friday, the ex-dividend date is Wednesday. If the record date is a Monday, the ex-dividend date is Thursday.*

COMPANIES RAISING THEIR DIVIDENDS

The payout ratio provides a clue as to the likelihood of a dividend increase.

The importance of dividends in a portfolio's total return is hard to overstate. Obviously, the greater the dividend growth from year to year, the greater the total-return possibilities.

How can an individual investor guess where big dividend increases will occur?

Since dividends are paid out of earnings, companies reporting strong earnings growth are good candidates to boost their dividends at above-average rates. Tracking corporate earnings is easy, because most companies report their quarterly profits in *The Wall Street Journal*.

Another method of picking issues with outstanding dividend-growth prospects is by examining payout ratios. A company's payout ratio is the annual dividend per share divided by the firm's latest 12-month earnings per share. This figure gives a comfort zone for future dividend payments. The lower the payout ratio, the more easily the dividend is paid out of current earnings.

Investors can then compare the current payout ratio with the firm's payout range over the last 5 or 10 years. If the payout ratio is on the low side of that range, the firm could be poised for a good dividend increase, particularly if earnings have been showing steady growth.

WHAT IS A STOCK'S YIELD?

Think of yield as similar to the interest rate earned on a bank savings account.

A stock's yield is determined by dividing the annual dividend per share by the stock price. Think of yield as similar to the interest rate earned on a bank savings account.

For example, if you have $200 in the bank earning 5 percent interest, you will receive $10 in interest for the year. Similarly, if you own a stock priced at $50 per share with a yield of 5 percent, you will receive $2.50 per share in dividends per year.

Another way to look at yield is the following: If a stock you own is trading at $25 per share and pays $1 per share in dividends per year, the yield is 4 percent (1 divided by 25 equals 0.04, or 4 percent).

Some investors use yield to pick stocks, while others ignore yield and focus on a company's capital-gains potential. Capital gains represent the rise in the stock price over time. One reason an investor may trade a higher yield for capital-gains potential is that long-term capital gains are taxed at a lower rate than dividend income for individuals in the highest tax bracket. Conversely, an investor who needs dividend income to supplement other forms of income may focus investments in higher-yielding stocks.

THE IMPORTANCE OF DIVIDENDS

A sizable dividend yield may act as a buffer during down markets.

A number of studies breaking down stocks' total return over time indicate that investors should give more than a passing thought to dividends. For example, for the 15-year period ending 1995, the Standard & Poor's 500 achieved a total return of 694 percent. Without reinvestment of the dividends, the gain was 354 percent.

Investing in good dividend-paying stocks is especially important during rocky market periods. An issue paying an above-average yield does not depend solely on capital gains to reward shareholders. In addition, a sizable yield may act as a buffer during weak markets.

Investors should remember that an exceptionally high yield may indicate a serious problem with the company. Thus, it is important to do your homework before investing in high-yielding stocks.

WHAT IS TOTAL RETURN?

Total return is the sum of a stock's price appreciation and dividend yield.

One problem investors encounter is determining how well their investments are doing. In order to evaluate the performance of a stock or portfolio, you must understand the concept of "total return." A stock's total return measures the entire gain or loss generated by the investment. Total return is simply the sum of a stock's price appreciation plus the stock's yield.

Let's say you own a stock trading at $50 at the beginning of the year. At the end of the year, the stock is trading for $75 per share. Furthermore, over the course of the year you receive $2 per share in dividends.

What's the stock's total return?

First, add up the stock's capital gains, and convert that to a percentage. In this example, the stock rose 25 points during the year, which translates to a 50 percent price appreciation (25 divided by 50 equals 0.50, or 50 percent). Also, you received $2 in dividends on your $50 investment, which translates to a yield of 4 percent. Add the yield to the price appreciation, and the stock's total return is 54 percent.

You can use a similar computation to figure out your portfolio's return. Say your portfolio begins the year at $25,000, and you add no new money during the year. At the end of the year, the portfolio has risen to $35,000. The increase includes dividends paid on your stocks that totaled $1,000. Thus, your portfolio's total return is 40 percent ($9,000 in capital gains plus $1,000 in dividends divided by $25,000).

How do you know whether a portfolio's yearly performance was good or bad? One way is to compare a portfolio's performance against a benchmark, such as the Standard & Poor's 500 index. If the portfolio's total return for the year is 10 percent, but the S&P 500 has a total return of 25 percent, your portfolio dramatically trailed the market.

What's a reasonable expectation for a stock portfolio's annual total return? Obviously, total return will vary greatly from one year to the next. However, it's useful to know that the average annual total return of the Standard & Poor's 500 since 1926 has been between 10 percent and 11 percent.

THE RULE OF 72

The "rule of 72" provides an easy tool to determine average annual market return.

If your portfolio doubled in value over the last four years, do you know what your average annual return was during those four years?

The "rule of 72" provides an easy tool to determine average annual market returns. The rule says the following: Take the number 72 and divide that by the number of years it took your portfolio to double (assuming you put no new money into the portfolio). That's your average annual return.

Let's return to our example. If you divide 72 by 4, the result is 18. The average annual return for a portfolio that doubles in four years is approximately 18 percent. What if your portfolio doubles every 10 years? Dividing 72 by 10 gives you 7.2. In other words, a portfolio or individual stock that doubles in value in 10 years has an average annual return of 7.2 percent.

You can use the rule of 72 to determine how long it will take a portfolio earning X amount each year to double. Say you have your funds in a money-market account earning 5 percent. By dividing 72 by 5, you know that it will take your funds a little over 14 years to double in value. What if you can increase your return to 8 percent? Your money now doubles in nine years.

One advantage of the rule of 72 is that it provides an easy way to gauge the value of boosting a portfolio's return an extra 1 or 2 percent each year. A portfolio that earns 9 percent a year doubles in eight years. A portfolio that increases an average of 10 percent per year doubles in a little over seven years.

The rule of 72 also makes it easy to put the stock market's long-term performance in perspective. Recall that the stock market's average annual return since 1926 is just under 11 percent—not the 15 percent, 20 percent, or 30 percent annual returns posted in the 1990s. Dividing 72 by 11 means that the stock market since 1926 has, on average, doubled every 6.6 years.

Keep that in mind the next time you start whining to your broker that it took a whole five years for your stocks to double in value. (What's a doubling in five years? An average annual return exceeding 14 percent.)

WHAT IS MARKET CAPITALIZATION?

Think of a stock's market capitalization in terms of how Wall Street is pricing the entire company.

If you had deep pockets and wanted to buy a publicly traded company, the first thing you'd want to know is the company's price tag. To determine the price tag, you need to know the company's market capitalization.

A firm's market capitalization is figured by multiplying the stock price by the number of outstanding common shares. For example, the market capitalization of a company with a stock price of $50 per share and 10 million outstanding common shares is $500 million ($50 times 10 million).

Remember that the value of a publicly traded company is ultimately determined by Wall Street. A good way to view a stock's market capitalization is to look at how Wall Street is pricing the entire company. A company with a market capitalization of $500 million means Wall Street believes the price tag for the entire firm is $500 million.

Now that you know what market capitalization means, it's easy to guess what small-cap stocks are. These are companies whose market capitalizations are between $250 million and $750 million. Conversely, big blue chips, such as the firms that are part of the Dow Jones Industrial Average, are large-cap stocks, with market capitalizations well into the billions of dollars.

WHAT IS A P-E RATIO?

The best way to interpret a stock's P-E ratio is as a popularity index.

A common tool investors use to evaluate a stock is a P-E ratio. The P-E ratio is a company's stock price divided by the 12-month earnings per share. For example, a company with earnings of $2 per share over the last 12 months and a stock price of $30 per share would have a price-earnings ratio of 15.

The best way to interpret a P-E ratio is as a popularity index. Stocks that are popular with investors sport high P-E ratios, while those that are in the doldrums usually carry lower P-E ratios. A company experiencing rapid earnings growth usually has a much higher P-E ratio than a company in a cyclical industry whose earnings have been volatile.

A number of studies suggest that stocks with low P-E ratios have some ability to outperform the market. The logic is that these stocks already discount the worst, and any positive earnings surprises drive them sharply higher. Conversely, stocks with high P-E ratios reflect high expectations and are vulnerable to sharp sell-offs should results come in below Wall Street's expectations.

I think the best way to use a P-E ratio is relative to the market and its historical range. For example, a stock with a P-E ratio that is usually above the market average but that has recently dipped below the market average may be a potential turnaround play. Also, a stock that normally trades with a P-E ratio at a 30 percent premium to the market P-E ratio but now is only at a 5 percent premium may signal a buying opportunity.

One rule of thumb many investors use is never to invest in an issue whose earnings growth rate does not match or exceed the P-E ratio. According to this thinking, a company with a 40 percent earnings growth rate could support a stock with a P-E ratio of 40 or under; a company with a 10 percent growth rate would be considered overvalued if its stock's P-E ratio was 20.

INFLATION AND P-E RATIOS

Low inflation usually translates into high P-E ratios.

To understand why low inflation is good for stocks (and high inflation is bad), it's important to under-stand the relationship between a stock's price-earnings ratio and inflation.

Inflation is a general rise in the price level. In a low-inflation environment, a dollar holds its value going forward. In a high-inflation period, a dollar's value erodes over time as a rising price level decreases the dollar's buying power.

Investors generally assign P-E ratios, in part, on the basis of a firm's earnings-growth capability. Companies expected to have fast-growing profits are generally afforded higher P-E ratios than stocks with modest growth prospects. Why? Because investors are willing to pay a premium for growth.

A P-E ratio reflects expectations for future earnings growth. The better the expected earnings growth, the higher the P-E ratio, all other things being equal. Now, what if inflation is running at high levels? In this scenario, the future earnings of a company are not going to be worth as much because of the effects of inflation. If the value of future earnings is expected to be affected adversely by inflation, then investors will not be willing to pay as much today for a company's future earnings. What that means in terms of a company's P-E ratio is that investors will not be as willing to assign high P-E ratios, since the value of the growth is discounted by inflation.

The upshot is that P-E ratios contract during periods of high inflation. During periods of low inflation, the future value of earnings retains its value, which means investors are willing to pay a premium for growth (or higher P-E ratios).

Once you comprehend the relationship between inflation and P-E ratios, it's easy to understand why inflation is so closely watched by investors. High inflation means contracting P-E ratios, which means lower stock prices. If inflation is low or falling, P-E ratios expand, which means higher stock prices.

WHAT IS A STOCK'S BOOK VALUE?

Many investors use book value as a benchmark for the company's underlying worth.

Book value is one of those terms that few investors understand and fewer know how to use when evaluating stocks. Book value is found by subtracting the company's liabilities from its assets and then dividing by the number of shares outstanding.

A company with assets of $5 million and liabilities of $3 million (these numbers come off a company's balance sheet) has a "net worth" of $2 million. If there are 1 million common shares outstanding, the book value is $2 per share ($2 million net worth divided by 1 million common shares).

Many investors use book value as a benchmark of the company's underlying worth and compare book value with the stock price to determine whether the stock is overpriced or underpriced. The problem with using book value in this way is that, in many cases, a company's assets are understated on the balance sheet.

For example, a company may have certain real estate

assets on its books at the firm's cost of acquisition. If the real estate was acquired many years ago, the real estate's value on the balance sheet may dramatically understate the real estate's current market value. In this scenario, the company's book value would understate the real value of the corporation if the firm's assets were liquidated. Thus, the stock may be trading significantly above the book value for good reason, since the stock price is more a reflection of the true value of the corporation.

When book value is used as a stock-pricing tool, it is important to look beyond the accounting numbers (that's all book value really is—an accounting device) and examine the true value of the assets and liabilities underlying the number.

STOCK SPLITS

Stock splits occur most often in the second quarter.

Stock splits are a popular event for investors. Perhaps it's the psychological effect of having more shares after the split that makes investors excited. However, much debate exists as to whether stock splits really benefit investors.

Some studies indicate that stocks rise following split announcements, at least for a short period of time. One rationale is that many companies announce stock splits at the same time that they announce dividend increases. The improved price action may be a response to the positive signal the company is sending through its dividend increase.

One study by the New York Stock Exchange provides an interesting link between stock splits and stock performance. According to the study, stocks that split increase in price 2.5 times faster than nonsplitting shares in the seven years surrounding the split. Most of the gains occur within three years of the split.

Another study by Ford Investor Services showed that a year after a 2-for-1 split, stocks have usually done 5.45 percentage points better than the overall stock market. A 3-for-2 stock split is almost as beneficial (4.39 percentage points). One interesting result of the study was that a 3-for-1 stock split had hardly any effect on the stock price.

When any such study is evaluated, it is important to separate cause and effect. Are these stocks moving higher because of the split? Or are they splitting because their strong earnings prospects have pushed the stocks higher? It's a hard case to argue, in my opinion, that a stock split has any effect on long-term performance. Stock splits result from a company's strong earnings momentum, which pushes share prices higher and into ranges where stock splits are likely.

If you still want to buy stocks in anticipation of splits, watch for certain patterns:

- Stock splits usually occur after a stock has made a big move.

- More than half of all stock splits occur in stocks

priced between $20 and $49, with the median price being $42.

- Stock splits occur most frequently in the second quarter, apparently after they are approved at annual meetings.

REVERSE STOCK SPLITS

Stock prices generally react negatively to a reverse stock split announcement.

One situation where a stock split is definitely bad news for investors is when companies enact "reverse" stock splits. For example, a company undergoing a 1-for-5 reverse stock split will exchange one share for every five shares held by an investor. An investor with 100 shares will have 20 shares after the reverse stock split.

Why do companies undergo reverse stock splits? One reason is that a reverse stock split automatically raises the price of a share. In our example, a $2 stock prior to the 1-for-5 reverse stock split becomes a $10 stock after the split. Higher-priced stocks are perceived to be of higher quality than lower-priced stocks. Pension funds and other institutional investors may not be permitted to invest in low-priced stocks, so companies undergo reverse splits to expand the potential market for their shares.

Another reason that companies undergo reverse stock splits is to escape the purview of regulators, who have cracked down on penny-stock scams. A stock trading for $1 may come under closer scrutiny by regulators than one trading for $10. Therefore, the company undergoes a 1-for-10 reverse stock split, and a $1 stock becomes a $10 stock.

Stock prices generally react negatively to a reverse stock split announcement, and the stock usually under-performs for a long time after the reverse split.

STOCK BUYBACKS

A company buying back its stock believes it's undervalued.

If you're looking for a bullish signal from a company, look at whether the firm is buying back its stock. Stock buybacks are perceived as favorable for several reasons:

- A company buying back its stock automatically lowers the number of outstanding shares, thereby boosting per-share profits.

- The fact that the company views its stock as a good investment is an indication that the stock is undervalued or at least attractively valued versus alternative investments the company could make.

- A company that is buying back its stock is, in effect, acting as a prop for the stock, since the company's buyback activities provide buying support.

Following the lead of companies that are buying back their stock is not a guarantee for profits. However, it is one factor that should carry extra weight when you are choosing new stock investments.

DUTCH AUCTION

Dutch auctions have become a popular tool for corporations to repurchase their own shares.

If your broker calls to say you've been invited to participate in a Dutch auction, it has nothing to do with bidding for a Van Gogh.

Dutch auctions have been a popular tool for corporations to repurchase their own shares. A company will buy back its stock primarily because it feels that the shares are undervalued. Traditional corporate buyback methods include open-market purchases as well as tender offers for a specific number of shares from shareholders at a fixed price.

In a Dutch auction, a company makes a tender offer for a specific number of shares. The difference is that instead of buying back the shares at a fixed price, the firm sets a price range for its buyback. Shareholders who participate must specify at what price in that range they are willing to sell.

The advantage for companies is that they usually are able to repurchase the shares at or near the low end of the price range. For shareholders, the deal often provides a way to sell the stock above the current market price without incurring commissions.

WHAT IS
THE DOW?

Higher-priced stocks carry greater weight in the Dow than lower-priced stocks.

The Dow Jones Industrial Average celebrated its hundredth anniversary in 1996. Despite being around for a century, the Dow Industrials are still a mystery to many investors. The following is a brief primer on the Dow:

• The Dow Jones Industrial Average made its debut May 26, 1896. The average was developed by Charles Dow, who cofounded Dow Jones & Co., the publisher of *The Wall Street Journal*. Initially, the Industrial Average comprised 12 companies. Only General Electric remains today from the original 12. On October 1, 1928, the Dow was expanded to 30 stocks.

• The prices of all 30 stocks are added together in order to compute the Dow each day. The sum is divided by the "divisor," which is, at the time of this writing, 0.29121. This divisor reflects adjustments to the prices of Dow stocks as a result of stock splits, spin-offs, and so on. If each Dow stock rose one point in a trading day, the Dow Jones Industrial Average would rise 103 points (30 divided by 0.29121). As you can see, as the divisor shrinks, the index potentially becomes more volatile. Indeed, the same one-point move in all 30 Dow stocks with a divisor of 0.2705 would result in a one-day jump in the Dow index of 111 points (30 divided by 0.2705).

- The Dow Jones Industrial is a price-weighted index; higher-priced stocks have greater weight in the average than lower-priced stocks. For example, a 10 percent move in a low-priced Dow stock, such as Wal-Mart Stores, does not have nearly the impact on the Dow relative to a 10 percent move in a high-priced Dow stock, such as Minnesota Mining & Manufacturing.

DAWN OF A NEW DOW

Investors who ignore the changing face of the Dow do so at their own peril.

You have to give it to the Dow Jones Industrial Average. This index, often scorned by market pros who consider it stodgy and old-fashioned, has been the best-performing index in recent years, rising 33 percent in 1995 and 26 percent in 1996.

One reason for the strength in the Dow relative to the glamour indices is that Dow stocks have been showing impressive earnings gains. These gains are due, in part, to an improving economy. Even more important, the Dow stocks, as a group, have been undergoing massive restructuring in recent years. The size and the extent of these restructurings have been minimized on Wall Street yet have had a monumental effect on the Dow's earnings growth, which is now being seen in quarterly corporate earnings reports.

To be sure, there are those analysts who say that the Dow Industrials are on borrowed time. While it may be true that the Dow could pull back in the near term, I think the prospects for continued gains over the next several years are quite good. Investors who ignore the changing face of the Dow and its implications for long-term performance do so at their own peril.

DOW'S FACE-LIFT

The new-look Dow will likely experience greater growth— but also greater volatility—over the next several years.

The Dow Jones Industrial Average received a face-lift in 1997. Four new companies—Travelers Group, Hewlett-Packard, Johnson & Johnson, and Wal-Mart Stores—were added to the index. Removed were Texaco, Bethlehem Steel, Woolworth, and Westinghouse Electric.

In looking at the switches, it's clear the changes were made partly to modernize the index. Most telling of all switches was the addition of Johnson & Johnson—a health-care company—at the expense of Bethlehem Steel—a steel company. The addition of Johnson & Johnson gives the index two health-care components (Merck & Co. is the other); the steel sector is no longer represented in the index.

Telling, too, was the addition of Hewlett-Packard—a technology stock—at the expense of Texaco, a major oil concern. Clearly, increasing representation of the all-important technology sector, at the expense of the old-line oil sector, gives the index a more modern look.

I also think the switches were a way to "juice" the index a bit. It's noteworthy that three of the four stocks that were removed from the index were trading below their 1991 highs. On the other hand, three of the four new stocks— the exception being Wal-Mart—have shown big gains in recent years.

Finally, it's important to remember that higher-priced stocks carry greater weight in the Dow than lower-priced stocks. So it's significant that three of the stocks that were replaced traded below $25 per share, while three of the four stocks that were added traded for more than $50 per share.

The upshot is that the new-look Dow is likely to show greater growth potential over the next several years. But that growth will likely be accompanied by greater volatility.

WHAT A DIFFERENCE A STOCK MAKES

If IBM had not been kicked out of the Dow in 1939, the Dow Industrial Average would be much higher.

Playing the "what if" game is a favorite investor pastime. "What if" I had bought $1,000 worth of

Microsoft at the end of 1986—the first year the company was publicly traded? That $1,000 would now be worth more than $92,000.

Here's a "what if" for you: What if IBM had not been kicked out of the Dow Jones Industrial Average in 1939? Where would the Dow be today?

The answer comes to us from the Institute for Econometric Research, based in Florida. In 1939 the people at Dow Jones & Co. replaced IBM (then known as International Tabulating) with AT&T. IBM remained out of the Dow until 1979, when it returned to the index. What was the effect of the AT&T-for-IBM swap? Had IBM remained a Dow component between 1939 and 1979, the Dow Jones Industrial Average would be approximately twice its current level.

If there's an investment lesson to be learned here, it's the following: Since Dow Jones & Co. makes such few changes in the index, when it throws in the towel on a stock and removes it from the index, perhaps that indicates the stock has reached rock bottom. I'm not suggesting that a winning portfolio strategy is to buy the castoffs of the Dow Jones Industrial Average. What I am saying is that such castoffs may represent interesting turnaround situations.

Among the four issues recently removed from the index—Bethlehem Steel, Westinghouse Electric, Woolworth, and Texaco—the one I find the most appealing from a turnaround standpoint (and the one I've been buying steadily over the last year or so) is Westinghouse. The firm has undergone a tremendous metamorphosis in recent years to become a pure play in the broadcasting industry. I think this change should lead to strong earnings growth over time and a much higher valuation on Wall Street.

STOCK SPLITS AND THE DOW

Stock splits of Dow components increase the average's volatility.

S tock splits have a potentially big impact on the Dow Jones Industrial Average, but you have probably never realized it.

The impact comes from the way the Dow Industrial Average is computed. Every day, the prices of the 30 Dow stocks are totaled, and that number is divided by a "divisor." As previously stated, this divisor takes into account stock splits, stock dividends, spin-offs, and other changes to the prices of Dow components.

The upshot is that every time a stock splits, the divisor is lowered. Lowering the divisor actually increases the volatility of the average.

Stock splits can also have a dampening effect on the Dow. Remember that the Dow Industrial Average is a price-weighted average. Since higher-priced stocks have a bigger impact on the average, stock splits in Dow components reduce the impact a stock will have on the average. Thus, a stock that has been performing well and has risen to high levels will see its influence on the Dow diluted when it splits.

THE MARKET AS A DISCOUNTING MECHANISM

The movement of the stock market reflects where the economy will be six months from now.

I always chuckle when I read that investors cannot understand why the market is behaving in a certain way given the economic climate. Part of the problem is that the press needs to know why; and quite frankly, sometimes analysts don't know why the market is behaving the way it is.

The stock market discounts everything, including the economy. Its movements reflect not what's happening in the economy today—the market reflected that three to six months ago—but where the economy will be half a year from now. That is why it is always dangerous to attach too much significance to current news when assessing the market situation.

This point is especially important in poor economic periods. During these times, you don't have to read too far in the daily paper to come across the comment: "The stock market won't go anywhere until more signs of an economic recovery are prevalent." I'm here to tell you that if you wait until the economy has recovered, it will generally be too late to catch the biggest gains in the stock market. Major market moves often precede the rebound in the economy by six months or so.

MARKET CORRECTIONS

A "correction" within a bull market usually lasts three weeks to three months.

When you hear your favorite stock market prognosticators talking about a market "correction," what they really mean is that stock prices are falling.

Corrections are part of all bull markets and should not necessarily be regarded as a bad thing for long-term investors. One purpose of a market correction is to relieve some of the speculative steam that builds up during extended market advances. By periodically relieving the pressure, corrections help sustain the life of a bull market.

Of course, all bear markets start as "corrections" within bull markets, and it's difficult to determine before the fact whether a market decline is a change in the market's primary trend. Fortunately, certain clues are often available to help investors determine whether a market plummet is a correction in a bull market or the beginning of a bear market:

- Corrections during bull markets are usually much more violent than the trading action during the preceding market advance. It is not unusual for the market to plunge sharply during a market correction. Conversely, bear markets generally start with a whimper, not a bang. Rare is the bear market that is kicked off by a plunging market. Bear markets usually take time to unfold and often sneak up on investors. If a market rises 10 percent in four months only to give back half or more of its gain in four weeks, chances are the decline is a correction within a bull market and not the beginning of a bear market.

- Corrections within bull markets generally last three weeks to three months.

- Corrections usually retrace one-third to two-thirds of the market advance since the last significant market low point. For example, let's say the Dow Jones Industrial Average, after bottoming at 20,000 (I can dream, can't I?), rises to 26,000 in a matter of 12 months (the dream continues). A bona fide market correction could be expected to drop the market at least one-third of the 6,000-point advance (or 2,000 points) and as much as two-thirds of the advance (or 4,000 points) in a period of three weeks to three months.

Being able to tell the difference between a correction in a bull market and the beginning of a bear market is important, since it will keep investors from selling stocks prematurely.

The best tactic during market corrections is not to try to time the decline by trading stocks, but to use the decline to acquire high-quality stocks that undergo short-term pullbacks.

ROTATIONAL CORRECTIONS

Rotational corrections affect only certain industry groups, not the entire market.

Most investors understand that a market correction means that the overall market, as measured by one of the popular indexes (the Dow Jones Industrials or S&P 500), falls. On the other hand, a rotational correction applies not to the overall market but to individual stock groups. Investors "rotate" out of leading industry groups (which then correct) and move their money into weak industry groups (which become the new leaders).

What is significant about a rotational correction is that it can serve the same purpose as a major market correction, in that both types of corrections help relieve the pressure that has built up in the market. However, rotational corrections, because they affect only certain industry groups rather than the entire market, are much less scary than market crashes and therefore are a more "investor-friendly" way for the overall market to remain healthy.

Given a market structure dominated by institutional investors and big mutual funds—entities which are loath to do aggressive, across-the-board selling of stocks—rotational corrections are likely to remain a primary method for this market to blow off steam.

I love rotational corrections since they can provide buying opportunities in solid growth stocks that momentarily fall out of Wall Street favor.

WHAT IS A BEAR MARKET?

The average bear market this century has lasted 17 months and declined approximately 30 percent.

Although it's been a while since a prolonged bear market has taken place, it probably wouldn't be a bad idea to do some freshening up on what occurs during bear markets.

While no two bear markets are alike, patterns have evolved since the turn of the century. For example, the average bear market this century has lasted roughly 17 months and declined roughly 30 percent. These are just averages, but the duration and severity of the typical bear market should give investors some cause for concern.

How have recent bear markets behaved? Extremely atypically. Analysts give many reasons for the "mini" bear markets of the recent past. The institutionalization of the markets and the growing use of options and futures are believed to have compressed declines into a shorter time frame. However, investors who believe that protracted bear markets are a thing of the past are in for a rude awakening. Given the strong markets over the last decade, it's growing increasingly likely that a protracted bear market will occur within the next five years.

WHAT IS PORTFOLIO DIVERSIFICATION?

You don't need to own 100 stocks to be properly diversified.

The benefits of diversification have been preached long and hard in the financial media.

"Don't have all your eggs in one basket" is the mantra of financial planners for their clients. "Better to diversify and spread out your risks." While it is tough to dispute the benefits of diversification, it is important to know just how much diversification is needed.

The mutual fund industry has done a masterful job of advertising that you need to hold literally hundreds of stocks to be properly diversified—thus the reason you need to own a mutual fund, which invests in hundreds of companies. However, studies have shown that you don't need to own 100 or more stocks to be diversified. A portfolio of 13 to 17 stocks, representing different industries, can provide most of the benefits of diversification that a portfolio of 100 stocks or more can provide.

Of course, a portfolio of 15 utility stocks is not my idea of being diversified. However, if stocks are picked from a variety of industries, a portfolio of 15 stocks can be adequately diversified while still being relatively easy to manage.

Proper diversification means including asset types that don't closely correlate with U.S. markets, such as foreign investments. Academic research has shown that including foreign investments enhances possible returns without increasing risk levels.

The next time you get steered out of owning individual stocks because of diversification considerations, remember that you may not need as many stocks as you think to be diversified.

WHAT IS ASSET ALLOCATION?

Asset allocation is the art of combining various types of investments into a single, well-diversified portfolio.

Asset allocation is like making a rum raisin pie. Not only do you need certain ingredients to make a superior rum raisin pie—raisins, rum, more rum, still more rum—but you also need to have the right amount of each ingredient. Too much or too little of any ingredient (did I say more rum?) can ruin a good pie.

Asset allocation takes various ingredients—stocks, bonds, mutual funds, cash, real estate—and attempts to combine them to achieve maximum expected profits with as little expected risk as possible. Academicians claim that more than 90 percent of a portfolio's expected return is generated by how assets are allocated rather than by the performance of each asset class. For that reason, it's important to pay attention to the percentage allocation of each of the investment classes in your portfolio.

If you are totally lost in terms of how to allocate assets, a fairly "neutral" asset allocation is 60 percent stocks (or stock mutual funds), 30 percent bonds (or bond funds), and 10 percent cash (money-market accounts, certificates of deposit, bank savings accounts, checking accounts, Treasury securities). This asset mix is a good place to start. If you are on the more aggressive side, add to your stock holdings and lower your bond holdings. If you are conservative, beef up your bond and cash percentages and reduce your stock allocation.

If you are still at a loss in terms of how to allocate your assets, a good rule of thumb is to subtract your age from 110; this is the percentage of assets that should be in stocks or stock mutual funds. A 60-year-old should feel reasonably comfortable having 50 percent (110 minus 60) of his or her assets in stock or stock equivalents.

Of course, when figuring your asset allocation, consider income level, retirement savings, risk aversion, financial responsibilities, and other factors that will affect your appropriate asset mix.

3

THE INDIVIDUAL
INVESTOR

The next time you read that the market is ready to tank because millions of "uneducated investors" are simply "throwing their money" at stocks and mutual funds, don't believe it.

I'm getting a bit tired of reading about how "stupid" small investors are and how the "smart" money on Wall Street likes to do just the opposite of the little guys. To be sure, there are many investors new to the stock market, forced into being their own money managers by virtue of managing their IRAs and 401(k) plans. Still, to paint all individual investors with the brush of stupidity is both demeaning and, in fact, stupid.

I maintain that never before has there been an investing public so attuned to the market. Thanks to the plethora of financial newsletters, magazines, newspapers, television and radio shows, and on-line financial advice, it has never been easier to become educated on investments. And millions of investors are availing themselves of this educational process. I meet literally thousands of investors each year through my newsletters and speeches throughout the country. What I see are small investors who increasingly understand market risk, who know the importance of diversification, and who are willing to look forward more than just the next week or month in order to achieve decent market returns.

Besides, if the "smart" money were so smart, how come more than two-thirds of diversified equity mutual funds—funds presumably in the hands of Wall Street's brightest—don't even match the performance of the S&P 500 in most years? Maybe Wall Street should spend less time focusing on the machinations of the "smart" money and more time doing what small investors are doing.

This chapter explores the individual investor and provides some helpful tips on, among other things, surviving and thriving on Wall Street.

OPPORTUNITIES FOR THE LITTLE GUYS

Wall Street's myopia spells opportunities for buy-and-hold investors.

With institutions dominating the market these days, is it even worth it for the little guy to buy stocks?

It may seem a bit one-sided in the stock market when institutional investors have the ability to move markets and virtually overrun individual investors. However, there are opportunities for investors who take advantage of the myopic tendencies of institutions. Indeed, with mutual funds and money managers having to produce top results on a quarterly basis to draw and keep money, institutional investors have become much more short-term oriented.

This shift has opened the door for individual investors who are looking to the long term and are willing to buy good stocks when they undergo periodic sell-offs. Though not glamorous, a buy-and-hold strategy has made many people rich, and the skittishness of the big guys should increase the opportunities for long-term investors.

THE "SPOILED" INVESTOR

Investors need to keep their expectations in check.

While I'm always glad to see stocks move higher, I'm often concerned that such strong market gains will only exacerbate what I see as a growing problem—the "spoiled" investor.

Market returns since 1982 have created a new breed of investor, one who believes that the only direction of stocks is upward and that there is no such thing as a loss. Unfortunately, financial markets, over time, give you the bad with the good. Despite a decade of stellar returns clouding our perception, the average annual return for stocks since 1926 isn't 20 percent, but less than 11 percent.

BOTTOM LINE: *Investors need to keep their expectations in check. Realize that stocks go down as well as up and that, at some point in the future, the market will likely show a poor performance for a two- or three-year stretch.*

INFORMATION OVERLOAD

Watching CNBC may be hazardous to your wealth.

Does it pay to read all the financial papers and magazines? To watch all the financial television shows?

To keep your eyes glued to the ticker tape? In other words, is an informed investor a profitable investor?

While I'm not willing to go out on a limb and say that "ignorance is bliss" when it comes to investing, I will argue that often investors suffering from information overload tend to make wrong investment decisions. Let's say you read in *The Wall Street Journal* that XYZ Corp. is a rumored takeover stock. You call your broker to buy 1,000 shares. Smart investor, right? Wrong. Acting on information that you read in the daily paper is one of the worst things you as an investor can do, since by the time you read the article the news is already reflected in the stock price.

Or consider investors who immerse themselves in so much minute-to-minute news that they become totally focused on the short run. Such myopic tendencies often make people lose sight of the big picture, the major trend, which usually results in selling stock prematurely. Investors need to keep in mind that successful stock market investing is a marathon, not a sprint, and reacting to every bit of new information is a good way to lose the race.

Granted, information is useful in the investing process, but it is what you do with the information that makes all the difference. Perhaps the biggest benefit of keeping abreast of things financial is that it helps you continually assess investment risk. Knowing how risky your investments are can pay dividends as you mold an investment program based on time horizons and income objectives.

QUICK TIPS FOR THE INDIVIDUAL INVESTOR

Don't chase yield.

Here are some quick tips for individual investors:

- Invest with your head, not your heart. Don't assume a stock that's been good in the past will be good in the future. Industry conditions change, and the formula that worked in the past may not work in the future. Continually evaluate the company's long-term prospects, its financial position, and its products' prospects.

- Don't be unduly influenced by the media concerning your investments. A number of times in the past the press just flat out reported an investment story wrong. Analyze all information first before taking action.

- Don't chase yield. This point is especially important. I'm afraid many investors moved money out of money markets and into stocks when yields fell sharply, not realizing the increased level of risk they assumed. Higher yields mean higher risk, so evaluate whether you want certain funds to be in more risky investments.

- Maintain discipline in your investment program, setting aside funds each month to invest.

- Leave market timing to the so-called experts. You're better off maintaining a consistent balance between equity and fixed-income investments, preferencing equities if you have a 10-year-plus investment horizon.

READING ANNUAL REPORTS

A number of companies include product discounts in their annual reports.

S pring is the time of year when shareholders' mailboxes get jammed with corporate annual reports. Unfortunately, in many cases, investors transfer the annual reports directly from the mailbox to the garbage can. Nevertheless, there are many reasons shareholders should read annual reports.

- It's your responsibility. Stock ownership cuts both ways, in my opinion. Shareholders have the right to be treated as owners. But shareholders also have the responsibility to behave like owners. That means taking an interest in the company's prospects, reading what your CEO has to say, examining the financial numbers. If you can't take 20 minutes to look at the annual report of a company in which you may have thousands of dollars invested, then you shouldn't complain when the stock tanks.

- You might actually learn something. For example, does

the firm have a new auditor this year? A company that changes auditors may be seeking a more sympathetic ear to try some accounting witchcraft to boost results. And how about the board of directors? Is it a good thing that 90 percent of them share the same last name? Merely the appearance of the report can provide useful information. Is it an expensive number with plenty of photos of top executives? Or is it a plain, no-nonsense report that gives the facts in a user-friendly way?

- You might save some money. A number of companies include product discounts right inside the annual report.

When the next annual report hits your mailbox, take a minute to look inside. You might be surprised at what you find.

THIS ORANGE WAS A LEMON

There are lessons to be learned from the Orange County financial debacle.

The 1994 financial debacle that occurred in California's Orange County holds a number of valuable lessons for the individual investor:

- *Stay within your risk parameters.* The money manager in Orange County was playing it fast and loose with taxpayers' money. Successful investors always decide how much risk they can assume and refuse to deviate from their stance.

- *Never chase yields.* One of the big allures of the Orange County fund for outside investors was that it was paying high yields. However, risk and return are joined at the hip; you can't have high expected returns without taking on greater risk. Smart investors use yield as a proxy for risk.

- *Don't believe your own press clippings.* It seems that the fund's manager was seen as a genius because of his strong performance prior to the fund's collapse. This may explain his unwillingness to alter his investment approach when interest rates began to rise in 1994. Maybe he believed he could do no wrong. Successful investors approach the market with humility.

- *Invest in what you know.* The Orange County fund manager invested in complex investments known as derivatives. Since few on Wall Street really understand these investments, that fund manager probably didn't either. Successful investors buy what they know and understand.

SHAREHOLDER ACTIVISM

It's easy for even small investors to have their voices heard.

A new sense of accountability is invading corporations these days thanks to the successful efforts of shareholder activists.

There was a time when shareholder activism centered primarily on social issues, such as military contracts and investments in South Africa. More recent shareholder activism has targeted areas more closely linked to stock performance as well as corporate governance. Now, shareholder activists want to hold corporate executives accountable for the stock's performance, and those companies that are failing to generate returns for shareholders are being targeted for revolt.

The revolts take several forms. Some activists demand meetings with management to express disappointment in the firm's performance. Shareholder activists also target agents of change, such as outside directors at various corporations, and attempt to influence these people to take a more active role in shaping corporate action. The success that shareholder activists have had at instigating changes at such companies as Sears, Westinghouse, and IBM will likely help the movement grow.

Interestingly, an investor doesn't have to have deep pockets or huge holdings of stock in order to have a say in corporate matters. Holding $1,000 worth of stock for

at least a year qualifies you to submit a shareholder pro-
posal to be considered at the annual shareholder meeting.

INVESTOR DON'TS

Don't buy a stock on a friend's "hot" tip.

The following is a list of investor don'ts that should
help steer you clear of some common pitfalls:

- Don't buy a utility just because it has a high yield.
  Many of the highest-yielding utilities are those with
  the greatest problems, and dividend cuts and omis-
  sions have been common among these utilities.

- Don't chase takeover stocks. Chasing takeover targets
  rarely pays off and usually results in buying an issue at
  the top. If you must play the takeover game, make
  sure you pick an issue that has long-term merit aside
  from takeover potential.

- Don't assume that a low-priced stock has limited
  downside risk. Even a $10 stock can be drastically
  overpriced.

- Don't buy a stock on a friend's hot tip. It's a good way
  to lose money and friends.

THE PERK OF EQUITY

Corporate chieftains have turned in their executive dining room privileges for stock options.

It used to be that what executives wanted were perks—the company car, country club membership, and executive washroom privileges. The perks of power.

Times have changed. Now everybody, from the top dog to the lowly clerk, wants only one perk—the perk of equity. This shift in emphasis from material to financial rewards has had a big influence on the stock market over the last five years. With corporate executives finally in the same boat as shareholders, it's no wonder that stock prices have been moving steadily higher.

Corporate executives now want what shareholders have always wanted—a higher stock price. And since the goals of the two groups are now aligned, corporations have been doing everything they can to increase stock prices. Often, this focus on stock price has resulted in "slash and burn" cost-cutting measures—draconian to many off Wall Street, but highly praised on Wall Street. This notion of increasing the stock price at all costs also has affected corporate America's willingness to boost dividends. Why pay out money to shareholders when the funds can be used to buy back stock—a tactic much appreciated by the market?

Of course, there are pundits who believe that the current "lift the stock price at any cost" mentality is myopic thinking at its worst. However, if a corporate executive's main job is maximizing shareholder value—which I think it is—it is hard to quibble with this paradigm shift among corporate bigwigs.

SHAREHOLDER PERKS

One way to judge how a company feels about its investors is by examining what perks and freebies are available to shareholders.

How a company treats its shareholders says a lot about the character of the firm and its management. Does the company perceive the shareholders, the true owners of the corporation, as important? Or are they considered nuisances?

One way to judge how shareholders rank with the company is by examining what perks and freebies companies make available to shareholders. Of course, these perks won't rank with company cars and planes, country club dues, stock options, and other perks available to top executives. Nevertheless, some companies know how to make a shareholder feel special.

For example, holders of at least one share of Anheuser-Busch Companies historically receive discounts of 15 percent at the firm's various entertainment and amusement parks, which include Busch Gardens, Sea World, Sesame Place, and Adventure Island. CSX, the railroad concern, is another company that provides perks for its shareholders. CSX's shareholders are entitled to discounts off accommodations at the company-owned Greenbrier Resort in West Virginia.

An academician would say that a discount or freebie is hardly a reason for an investor to buy stock in a particular company, and I would concur. Nevertheless, discounts on products or other shareholder perks may provide the final piece of the puzzle when two companies have the same total-return potential.

HOLIDAY PERKS

A number of companies play Santa around the holidays by giving their shareholders certain perks and freebies.

A number of companies shower holiday spirit on their shareholders.

For example, Brown-Forman, the maker of spirits and consumer products, traditionally gives shareholders discounts on various products around Christmas. One recent freebie was a 50 percent discount on the company's Hartmann luggage.

Wrigley (Wm. Jr.), the chewing gum company, makes Christmas a bit cheerier by giving each of its shareholders a box containing 20 packs (100 sticks) of gum. The flavor is chosen each year by the CEO.

A big holiday perk in dollar terms is offered by Tandy, the operator of Radio Shack stores. The firm gives shareholders a 10 percent discount on holiday purchases up to

$10,000. Thus, if you plan to load up on electronic gear this Christmas, it may pay to own Tandy stock and save up to $1,000.

A SHAREHOLDER PERK FOR THE PALATE

Shareholders of Chalone Wine Group receive discounts on top-shelf wines.

One of the more interesting shareholder perks is offered by Chalone Wine Group, a Nasdaq-traded company. Chalone holds stakes in 11 world-class wineries in the United States, France, Chile, and Portugal. Chalone shareholders with 100 shares or more are entitled to the following perks:

- Discounts of up to 25 percent on wine purchased from the company, including older-vintage, limited-quantity, and special-reserve bottles
- An invitation to enjoy, at a nominal fee, a luncheon accompanied by a collection of fine wines
- VIP tours of sites and vineyards, including, when available, tours of Chateau Lafitte-Rothschild
- An invitation to participate in shareholder dinners hosted by company executives at leading restaurants throughout the country
- The opportunity to use the firm's entertainment facilities for private dinners and parties

Wine connoisseurs may find the 100-share price tag (roughly $1,200, based on the stock's price at the time of this writing) a real bargain given the good deals available. Chalone sends a catalog each year to shareholders with discounts on a variety of bottles. And if you chug instead of sip, the wines can be purchased by the case.

Of course, the bottom line with any investment is the quality of the stock, and Chalone has been an inconsistent performer through the years. Nevertheless, I wonder how many of Chalone's shareholders who take advantage of the discounts even care that the stock hasn't been the second coming of Microsoft. My guess is very few.

For further information about Chalone's shareholder perk program, call (707) 254-4200.

PERKS OF CONVENIENCE

Safekeeping services and direct deposit of dividends are two helpful shareholder perks.

A number of companies make things easier for their shareholders by offering perks geared toward shareholder convenience.

For example, many firms provide certificate safekeeping services for shareholders. Usually, these services are an offshoot of the firm's dividend reinvestment program. Safekeeping services provide a number of benefits. First, lost or stolen certificates are eliminated. Also, investors won't have to pay the bank for a safety deposit box to store certificates. Most companies provide safekeeping services for no charge, and those that do charge usually have a nominal fee, often $5. To see if a firm in which you own stock offers safekeeping services, call the shareholder services department.

Another feature that appears to be growing in popularity is direct deposit of dividends. Direct deposit may save you from losing your dividend check, or at the very least save you from making a trip to your bank. Check with the shareholder services department to see if direct deposit is available.

COMPANY TOURS AND MUSEUMS

Corporate tours and museums provide an enjoyable, educational, and inexpensive outing for the whole family.

An excellent outing for you and your family is taking a company plant tour or visiting one of the many corporate museums throughout the United States. Some popular tours and corporate museums include the Chocolate World tour at Hershey Foods' headquarters in Hershey, PA; the Anheuser-Busch tour at the firm's St. Louis, MO headquarters; the Harley-Davidson tour at its motorcycle assembly facility in York, PA; and the Motorola Museum of Electronics in Schaumburg, IL.

Such tours give the visitor a fresh perspective on what it took to develop some of this country's premier companies. During an era when it has become fashionable to bash American manufacturing, seeing how Hershey Foods produces its chocolate or how Harley-Davidson makes its prized machines can instill a new appreciation for American ingenuity.

The tours and museums are interesting educational experiences for children as well. The Motorola Museum has a variety of interactive displays that help teach youngsters various properties of electricity and electronics. Perhaps best of all, most tours and museums are free to the public, making them excellent side trips during a family vacation.

KEEPING GOOD INVESTMENT RECORDS

The essence of good record keeping is keeping track of the "cost basis" of your investments.

I nvesting requires record-keeping disciplines. Brokers, transfer agents (the entities that administer company dividend reinvestment plans), and mutual funds make it easy for investors to keep track of their investments by sending regular statements showing an investor's trading history and current investment holdings. Still, if you throw those statements into the garbage, you might find yourself in a world of pain down the road, especially if you decide to sell stock.

When you sell stock, you have to account for the sale on your income taxes. To determine if you have a gain or a loss on the sale, you need to know what you paid for the stock. When you buy shares, your brokerage statement will show you exactly what you paid for the stock. This is important, since it represents the "cost basis" you will use when you sell shares.

The cost basis may change over time, depending on whether the stock splits or the company spins off certain assets. Let's say you buy 100 shares of McDonald's for $50 per share. Your cost basis is $50. Now, let's say McDonald's splits its stock 2 for 1. Following the split, you need to adjust for the cost of the additional shares. The stock split lowers your cost basis to $25 per share.

The essence of good record keeping is really keeping track of the cost basis of your investments.

When you sell shares of stock, you can use either the specific-share method or the first-in, first-out method. The specific-share method lets you use the specific cost that you purchased shares of stock as the cost basis. Let's say that you've made three purchases of McDonald's stock: a 100-share trade for $50 per share, a 100-share trade for $40 per share, and a 100-share trade for $60 per share. Under the specific-share method, if you sell 100 shares of stock, you can choose any of the 100-share purchase prices for your cost basis. In most cases, you'll choose the highest-cost shares, since this would lower your gain and therefore lower the potential capital-gains tax. On the other hand, you could choose the first-in, first-out method, which means that you would use the cost of the first shares you purchased (in this case, $50 per share) as your cost basis.

A number of computer software packages (many investors use Quicken) and manual record-keeping systems (my firm sells an excellent manual system) can assist investors in tracking their investments. Given the importance of keeping good records, investing in a record-keeping system is money well spent.

SO YOU WANT TO START AN INVESTMENT CLUB

A good place for information on investment clubs is the Michigan-based National Association of Investors Corporation.

It's official: There are now more investment clubs than people in China.

Investment clubs have been springing up in recent years at a growth rate exceeded only by the number of lawyers and bankers going to jail. Investment clubs just for women; clubs just for teens; clubs just for seniors; clubs for jailed lawyers and bankers—you name the demographic group, and chances are an investment club exists which caters to it.

Several factors are behind the immense growth in investment clubs. Obviously, the extended bull market has spurred interest in stocks, which has in turn spurred interest in investment clubs. The notoriety of the "Beardstown Ladies," an investment club consisting of grandmothers who claim to beat the market, has sparked interest, too. Perhaps the biggest factor is that we Americans like to turn everything into a social event— and that includes stock investing.

I've always been a bit leery of the concept of an investment club. My experience has been that when friends, avarice, and money mix, the combination is rarely a pleasant experience. For that reason, here are Carlson's rules for starting an investment club:

- Don't let anyone who shares your last name into the club.

- Don't let anyone who shares your maiden name into the club.

- Don't let your best friend into the club.

- Don't let your treasurer be anyone who ever handled money for Orange County, CA.

- Don't let your treasurer be anyone who has a bank account in the Cayman Islands and lots of frequent-flier miles.

- Don't let your boss into the club.

- Don't let your boss's spouse into the club.

- Don't let a broker into the club.

If there's anyone left and you'd still like to start an investment club, a good place for information is the

National Association of Investors (810-583-6242). This Michigan-based corporation provides plenty of useful stuff on starting and running a club, as well as worthwhile advice on picking stocks.

BEWARE OF BIG NUMBERS

When you hear big numbers thrown around in the media, don't be afraid to question the veracity of the numbers.

Occasionally you'll hear a stock-market analyst predict that the Dow Jones Industrial Average could go to 14,000 over the next 10 years. Pie-in-the-sky thinking? Not really.

If you earn just 7 percent a year on your money, your money will double in 10 years. Thus, a doubling of the Dow Industrials in 10 years implies a 7 percent average annual return. In those terms, a move to 14,000 is not only possible but expected.

This example brings up the problems that some individuals, not to mention business media, have with numbers, especially big numbers. I can't tell you how often I receive calls from nervous investors ready to dump the stock of a billion-dollar company because they heard on the local news that the company lost a lawsuit for $5 million. Quite frankly, $5 million to a company with billions in sales is virtually meaningless to the stock's investment prospects.

When you hear numbers being thrown around by analysts, friends, or the press, don't be afraid to question the veracity of the numbers. Chances are, there's probably more to the story.

BE CAREFUL WITH ON-LINE INFORMATION

Investors should not take for granted the truthfulness of information found in cyberspace.

Since information is power in the investment game, all investors owe it to themselves to explore the world of on-line services offered by Prodigy, CompuServe, and America Online. These three computer on-line services offer a variety of information that can be quite helpful in developing a profitable investment program. And for those investors who venture onto the Internet, the possibilities are endless.

What's available in cyberspace? All the services offer various "chat lines" for investors to bounce ideas off one another along with investment forums in which financial and investment publications make information readily available. Each of the on-line services also has various "expert" areas where individuals help answer questions. For example, I'm the dividend reinvestment plan expert for the *Motley Fool* personal finance forum found in America Online.

While these services are all potentially helpful, I think the biggest benefit is the wealth of information and research reports at investors' fingertips. Need to find the latest government employment report? It's available in cyberspace. Need to retrieve news on your stock holdings? Just use one of the many news search engines to find information. Want to find out what companies are leading exporters of a certain product? It's all there in cyberspace. (I'll provide you with some web sites later in this book.)

Of course, as with any other information source, investors need to examine closely the veracity of the information. Are the folks on the "chat line" giving you straight information, or do they have their own agenda for floating that takeover rumor? Is the anonymous response to your question being given by a broker who has a large position in the recommended stock?

It's up to you to be responsible for checking out the information before acting on it. Still, as an inexpensive information resource, the information highway is hard to beat.

DO YOU WANT TO BE PATRICK EWING'S BOSS?

A way exists for individual investors to own a small piece of a professional sports franchise.

Have you ever dreamed of being an owner of a professional sports team? Fortunately, there's a way for those of us who don't have deep pockets to own a small piece of a professional sports team by owning stock in publicly traded companies that own sports franchises.

- Want to be Patrick Ewing's boss? You can if you own stock in ITT Corporation, an owner of Ewing's New York Knicks basketball team and the New York Rangers hockey team.

- Or perhaps you'd rather be a baseball owner? All you need to do is own shares in Tribune Company (Chicago Cubs) or Coors (Adolph) (Colorado Rockies).

- For another basketball franchise, consider the Boston Celtics Limited Partnership (Boston Celtics).

- An unusual member of this fraternity is Walt Disney, which is the owner of the Anaheim Mighty Ducks, an NHL franchise, and the Anaheim (formerly California) Angels major league baseball franchise.

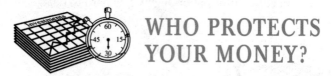

WHO PROTECTS YOUR MONEY?

Depositors with accounts greater than $100,000 should no longer expect to be bailed out entirely if their banks go under.

You should know the rules regarding insurance for your savings accounts. The most familiar insurance agency is the Federal Deposit Insurance Corp. (FDIC), which insures most banks. Under the FDIC, deposits are insured up to $100,000 per bank account. If you have $200,000 in your savings and checking accounts combined, this is considered one account, and you are insured only up to the $100,000 limit. IRAs are considered second accounts and are insured separately up to $100,000.

In many bank failures of the past, accounts that exceeded $100,000 were paid off in full. Depositors should not expect this to be the case in the future. The best way to get around the restrictions is to open separate accounts in different banks.

Other primary insurers of funds are the Securities Investor Protection Corporation (SIPC) and the National Credit Union Administration. The SIPC, a nonprofit organization, is the insurance body for the brokerage industry. The SIPC is not as comprehensive as the FDIC. Although it protects accounts against bankruptcies of brokers, it does not protect against fraud and deceptive selling practices which can fleece an investor. SIPC coverage limits are $500,000 in securities, including $100,000 cash. Many SIPC members carry additional insurance for depositors.

The National Credit Union Administration is a government agency which provides insurance for roughly 90 percent of all credit unions. As with the FDIC, deposits are insured up to $100,000 per account.

JUDGING THE SAFETY OF YOUR BANK

The stock price of your bank is an effective tool for measuring its health.

How can you tell if your bank is healthy?

Fortunately, there are some things you can do to monitor the health of your bank. First, check its credit rating. Moody's and Standard and Poor's are two services that rate financial institutions, and you should be able to find their ratings at your local library. Veribanc, a leading bank-rating agency, will give you a rating of an institution's finances over the telephone for $10. Call them at (800) 442-2657.

Another way to check on your bank is to examine the stock price of the parent company. Not all banks are publicly traded. For those that are, the stock price is an excellent indication of the bank's health. A stock price that has dropped dramatically or a dividend that has been omitted may signal a bank that is in bad shape.

HOW HEALTHY IS YOUR INSURANCE COMPANY?

A stock price that is in a nosedive often indicates an insurance firm on shaky ground.

A number of ways exist to evaluate the health of your insurance firm. One quick way is to examine the stock price, if your insurance firm is publicly traded. A stock price that is in a nosedive often indicates an insurance firm on shaky ground.

Another way is to get a professional opinion from one of the services which rates insurance firms. A leader in this field is A. M. Best Company. It's rating guide is considered must reading for individuals who would like to know how their insurance firm stacks up in the industry. In addition to its guide, A. M. Best offers a service, BestLine, which features Best's ratings for 3,800 property/casualty and life/health insurance concerns. BestLine can be reached by dialing (800) 424-2378. The caller must have either the A. M. Best Company identification number or the National Association of Insurance Commissioners (NAIC) identification number for each insurance company. The NAIC identification numbers may be obtained from state insurance departments. The price of the call is $2.95 a minute.

UNCLAIMED $$$$

The easiest way to avoid having your assets escheated to the state is by making sure your financial intermediaries have your current address.

Billions of dollars in assets are unclaimed in this country. The abandoned assets result from dormant checking and savings accounts, uncashed money orders and dividend checks, unclaimed insurance benefits, forgotten safekeeping depository contents, and unclaimed security deposits. The funds are often left by individuals who die and fail to account for the funds in their wills.

Under state laws holders of unclaimed property, such as banks, insurance companies, mutual funds, brokerage firms, and transfer agents, must try to find the rightful owners. If they can't, the money is eventually turned over (or "escheated") to the states' abandoned property divisions. It is up to these divisions to try to track down the rightful owners. The departments do so by posting notices in newspapers and running public service announcements.

Various procedures and forms need to be followed and filed in order to claim assets. If you believe you may be entitled to assets that either you or a relative has left unclaimed, contact the state agency responsible for its administration (usually it's the Department of Revenue's Unclaimed Property Division).

Of course, the easiest way to avoid having your assets escheated to the state is to make sure your financial intermediaries have your current address. Also, returning proxy statements is an excellent way to make sure your broker or transfer agent has an accurate address. Finally, make a complete record of all your financial holdings and the intermediaries administering the various accounts, and tell a family member or friend where this information can be found in case the records are needed.

TRACKING DOWN OBSOLETE SECURITIES

A few ways exist to check if those stock certificates you found in the attic are worth anything.

I t has been keeping you up at night.

"I wonder if those stock certificates I found in Aunt Bea's attic are worth anything?"

Relax. Ways exist to check if you're sitting on a fortune.

The first place to go is the stock-quote pages of *The Wall Street Journal* to see if the stock certificates belong to a company that is still trading on the New York, American, or Nasdaq stock exchanges.

If you come up dry here, you do have another alternative—but it will cost you money.

R. M. Smythe & Co. specializes in providing information, for a fee, on obsolete securities. The firm can be reached at 26 Broadway, New York, NY 10004 or by calling (212) 943-1880.

IT'S BETTER THAN AN UGLY TIE

Some companies make it especially easy to give the gift of stock.

If you're like me, you're finding it more difficult with every passing year to find that perfect birthday or holiday gift for your child, spouse, relative, or work associate. And you're probably finding the time to search for the perfect gift more scarce as well.

How about giving something this holiday season that can make a real difference in someone's life, both now and for years to come?

"What gift?" you ask. How about the gift of stock.

Think about it for a minute. Wouldn't you love to help a granddaughter fund her college education? It's possible with stocks. Or perhaps you have a friend who is a motorcycle enthusiast. Why not buy him Harley-Davidson stock?

You don't have many opportunities to effect meaningful change in people's lives. By starting a friend or a loved one on the road to investing with a gift of stock, you can make a big difference in that person's long-term financial well-being. Some companies make it especially easy to purchase stock as gifts. For example, Texaco (800-283-9785) has a gift-giving feature available for investors.

Instead of buying that ugly tie for your father or that overpriced sweater for your son or daughter, why not give the gift that keeps on giving year after year? Give stock this holiday season.

4

YOU AND
WALL STREET

An essential concept to understand in investing is that investment returns and risk are joined at the hip. All things being equal, you cannot get higher returns without incurring a higher level of risk.

There is one exception to this rule. Since portfolio returns are affected by transaction costs, holding down the costs of investing is one way to generate higher returns without assuming higher risk. What are these transaction costs? Brokerage commissions. Load fees. Redemption fees. 12b-1 fees. Administrative fees. Management fees. In short, any fees charged by brokers and mutual funds for investing or managing your money.

You might be wondering at this point what difference saving 1 or 2 percent a year in commissions and fees can do to a portfolio.

You'd be amazed.

Oh, sure. When portfolios were rising 18 percent or more annually in the 1980s and most of the 1990s, nobody cared about paying a few percentage points in commissions. However, with stocks more likely to return to their long-run average of roughly 10 percent to 11 percent annually, saving 1 or 2 percent a year can make the difference between a profitable portfolio and a losing one.

Say the market rises 8 percent in one year and inflation is 4 percent. That means that the after-inflation return on your investment is 4 percent, and that's before any taxes. Now, if you're paying 2 percent in fees for the year, that means that your return is a measly 2 percent before taxes. If you can save the 2 percent, you roughly double your pretax return.

Bottom line: Fees matter, so pay attention to how much you're paying to buy stocks and mutual funds.

This chapter examines ways to interact with Wall Street and your broker or financial institution in order to maximize portfolio profits while minimizing transaction costs.

SHOPPING FOR THE LOWEST BROKERAGE COMMISSIONS

In some cases, full-service brokers might have lower commissions than discounters.

Finding the lowest commission rates among brokers is not as easy as you would think. I've talked with brokers within the same brokerage firm who charge different rates. Furthermore, some brokers may charge modest commissions but have add-on fees, such as an extra charge to have the stock registered in your own name rather than "street" name. (Street-name registration means the shares are registered in the name of the brokerage firm.)

Don't assume from the label of discount broker that the fees are going to be low. Wide disparity in commission rates exists between discounters. And don't assume that a full-service broker will always have the highest commission rates.

My experience has been that full-service brokers, especially Dean Witter and A.G. Edwards, have exceptionally low commission rates for small-share purchases. In many cases, it is cheaper to buy a few shares of stock through a full-service broker than a discount broker. Full-service brokers have more latitude in their ability to cut commission rates, especially if they smell bigger business down the road. On the other hand, the minimum commission rate for most discounters seems to be set in stone, whether you buy 1 share or 100 shares.

If you have deep pockets and generally buy stock in big bunches, you're probably better off going through a discount broker. Kennedy, Cabot & Co. (800-252-0090), located in California, charges $23 to purchase 1 to 99 shares of stock. The firm does not charge an add-on fee if you want the shares registered in your own name.

The best way to shop for the lowest commission rates is to determine how many shares you plan to purchase of a particular stock and then make some phone calls to full-service and discount brokers.

ONE FINAL WORD: *If you feel you've paid too much in commissions following a trade, complain to the broker or the broker's boss. I have done this and have been successful in getting the fee lowered.*

BROKER "NO COMMISSION" TRADING PLANS

Firms may sell you shares from inventory for no commission because they want to unload the stock.

Perhaps some of you have seen those advertisements stating that certain brokerage firms will trade 1,000 shares of stock or more for you and not charge you a cent in commissions.

How can brokerage firms charge no commissions and keep their doors open?

One way is that the deal may be offered only on stocks "recommended" by the firm. In this case, it's quite possible that the firm maintains an inventory of the stock and may be looking to unload the shares on investors. If the company acts as a market maker, it can make money on the spread between the "bid" and "ask" prices even if it does not charge a commission.

Does that mean that the investor is getting a bad deal? Not necessarily. Still, investors who take up brokerage firms on the deal need to monitor the bid and ask prices to make sure that the spread is not unusually wide. Also, investors should not purchase a stock merely because the trade is commission free. The overriding factor in any buy decision should be the quality of the stock.

BROKER ORDERS

You have flexibility when making buy and sell orders through your broker.

When you buy and sell stocks through your broker, you can give specific instructions on how you want the shares bought and sold. The following are various broker orders when buying and selling stock:

- *Limit order.* A limit order is an order to buy the stock at a specific price. Let's say IBM is trading for $70. You don't want to buy the stock at $70 per share, but you would buy the stock at $68. You submit a "limit" order at $68 with your broker. Your limit order will not be filled unless IBM falls to $68 or lower.

- *Market order.* This type of order is the most common but perhaps the most dangerous, depending on the stock and how frequently it trades. A market order says that you are willing to buy the stock at the "best price" the broker can get at that moment. Depending on the stock, I've seen many individuals get skinned placing market orders. If a stock does not trade frequently, an investor may end up buying the stock with a market order at a price that seems far above the last trade. My suggestion is that, if you want to place a market order, find out the prevailing price first. Then, instead of placing an open-market order, make it a limit order based on the latest market price.

- *Day or good-until-canceled orders.* A day order is good for that day of trading. Let's say you place a limit order to buy IBM at $68, but the stock never trades that low during the day. If it's a day order and is never filled, the limit order will cancel at the end of the day. If you have a good-until-canceled order, the limit order will continue to be in effect until either the order is filled or you tell your broker to cancel.

- *Stop-loss order.* A stop-loss order sets a selling price below the current price. Stop-loss orders are used to protect profits. Let's say you own IBM at $70, and the stock has risen to $140. You are getting concerned about the market and want to protect your large profits in IBM. You call your broker and place a stop-loss order on IBM at $135. This means that if IBM falls to $135, you automatically sell your shares. When a stop-loss order is filled, it is referred to as getting "stopped out" of your stock.

Be careful when using any orders. I've seen people put limit orders one-quarter point below the market price only to see the stock skyrocket, leaving the investors behind. Don't "nickel and dime" your way into a stock. Pay the one-quarter point if it means you're assured of buying the stock. Don't lose out on a stock because you were trying to save 25 cents per share.

Likewise, go easy on stop-loss orders. I've seen investors set snug stop-loss orders that were filled on a minor blip downward in the stock price. Following the brief decline, the stock rallied and went on to post huge gains.

WHAT IS BUYING STOCK ON MARGIN?

Need money to buy stocks? Just ask your friendly broker.

Brokers are allowed to loan investors up to 50 percent of the purchase price of stock. The 50 percent that is put up by the investor is called "margin." Investors use margin to leverage their investments in stocks.

Let's say you buy 100 shares of a $50 stock. The investment would normally cost you $5,000. But you have a margin account with your broker that allows you to put up half the amount to cover the $5,000 investment. The broker doesn't loan you this money out of the goodness of his or her heart. As is the case with any loan, you'll pay interest. An investor using margin believes that gains in the investment will more than offset the interest on the loan.

Continuing our example, say the stock rises 20 percent to $60 per share, giving your shares a value of $6,000. Remember, however, that you didn't invest $5,000, but just $2,500. So what appears to be a gain of 20 percent on your investment is really a 40 percent gain ($1,000 divided by your $2,500 investment). Of course, the interest you paid on the margin loan will lower your return a bit. Nevertheless, from this example you can see the power of using margin in an investment program.

Of course, leverage cuts both ways. What if the stock in our example falls by 50 percent to $25 per share? Chances are you would have been hit with a "margin call." A margin call is a demand from a broker to put up money or securities when equity in a margin account declines below a minimum standard set by the exchange or the firm.

BOTTOM LINE: When you bet right using margin, you can win big by using borrowed funds to buy your investments. When you bet wrong, however, the penalty can be rather severe. For that reason, buying on margin is considered a risky investment strategy for nonprofessionals.

COLD-CALL COWBOYS

An easy way to handle unwanted broker cold calls is simply to hang up.

The securities industry makes an estimated 6 million calls a day in its pursuit of new business. That translates into 1.5 billion telemarketing calls a year, or an average of 80 calls per stockbroker per day. These startling numbers come from a report compiled by a congressional subcommittee on telecommunications and finance. The report, summarized in a story appearing in *Redemption Digest* and *Securities Industry Daily*, claims that one firm had 221 registered cold callers making an average of 150 to 200 calls per person per day.

While the subcommittee report acknowledged that the estimates were based on limited data—most brokerage firms surveyed, understandably, did not provide figures for the number of calls made—the report clearly provides evidence of what individual investors have known for some time: Cold-call cowboys in the brokerage industry are still burning up the phone lines.

How can you handle cold callers? One way is to make it clear you are not interested and demand to be put on the brokerage firm's "do-not-call list."

Another strategy is to do what the chairman of the Securities and Exchange Commission, Arthur Levitt, does when he receives unwanted cold calls from brokers.

He lies.

According to a *Barron's* article, Levitt says that he tells cold callers that he already has an account with their firm, making them feel silly for not knowing.

While I admire Mr. Levitt's ingenuity, there's an even easier way to fend off cold-call cowboys.

Simply hang up.

CHECKING UP ON YOUR BROKER

A few phone calls could help keep you out of trouble.

For investors who are willing to make a few phone calls, there is a way at least to lower the probability that your broker is hustling you.

The National Association of Securities Dealers records disciplinary actions by various securities regulators as well as criminal convictions. A quick call here may provide some pertinent information. The toll-free number is (800) 289-9999.

Another source for background information is the North American Securities Administrators Association. To find out who handles requests in your state, call (202) 737-0900.

If you're active in the commodities market, call the National Futures Association's Disciplinary Information Access Line (DIAL) at (800) 676-4632.

Remember that a clean slate at these sources doesn't

necessarily mean that your broker is clean. Current complaints may not be registered, and information is sometimes incomplete. Nevertheless, the phone calls are toll free in most instances. It's cheap insurance, and insurance you really can't afford to be without.

BROKERS AND HOUSE PRODUCTS

Brokers often generate fatter profits from house products.

An interesting court case reported in the financial press a few years ago provides insight into the inner workings of brokerage firms.

The case involved brokers at PaineWebber Group who accused the firm of forcing them from their jobs after the brokers balked at selling PaineWebber proprietary products to their clients.

Brokerage firms often generate fatter profits from the sale of "house" products.

The case was filed by five former brokers in PaineWebber's Tampa office. The brokers said that PaineWebber wanted them to sell products that the brokers felt were not suitable for many of their clients. The brokers claimed that PaineWebber forced them from their jobs because they refused to push these products. In a decision by an arbitration panel of the National

Association of Securities Dealers, PaineWebber Group was ordered to pay the brokers $700,000.

MORAL OF THE STORY: *Always know what products your broker is buying for you, and make sure that broker isn't fattening his or her wallet at the expense of your portfolio holdings.*

LIAR, LIAR

Beware of brokerage analysts bearing recommendations—a hidden agenda might exist.

H ere are a few conflicts of interest that could poison a Wall Street research report's objectivity:

- It's a fairly common practice among brokerage firms to write a report on a company that the broker has just "taken public" in an initial public offering. When a brokerage firm releases such a report, remember that it is in the best interest of the broker to keep the stock price of the newly issued shares as high as possible following the offering.

- Most Wall Street analysts are expected to help drum up stock underwriting business for the investment banking arms of their firms. Since a company is unlikely to do business with a Wall Street firm whose analyst bad-mouths the company in a negative research report, "sell" recommendations on Wall Street are about as common as a visit from Hale-

Bopp. What you have are hundreds of "buy" recommendations coming out of Wall Street and precious few "sell" recommendations, a practice that dilutes the real value of any recommendations to buy.

- Some brokerage firms carry inventories of stocks and bonds. If the firm wants to unload some of its inventory—perhaps the broker fears a bear market—it might issue a bullish research report on the companies whose stocks or bonds are in its inventory. The report helps boost the price, thus giving the broker a more attractive price at which to dump the stocks or bonds.

As a rule, the Wall Street recommendations that merit attention are the few sell recommendations that are issued in the course of a year. Since sell recommendations are generally higher-risk endeavors for Wall Street firms, a broker who gives a sell recommendation probably has done a lot of homework and is less encumbered by potential conflicts of interest.

CHOOSING AN INVESTMENT ADVISER

Word of mouth is often an effective way to find a trustworthy investment adviser.

Perhaps you're the lucky winner of the Publishers Clearinghouse sweepstakes and need help planning your financial future. Or you're a recent retiree with more cash than you've ever had in your life but no idea where to put it. Or perhaps you're just someone long on dough but short on time who would rather chip golf balls than study stocks.

Many Americans are turning to investment advisers to handle their financial affairs. One reason is that you no longer need to be a Rockefeller to have your own financial adviser. With an estimated 24,000 registered investment advisers working today, it's never been easier to find someone to take your money management needs off your hands.

Of course, the trick is to find one of the few good advisers among the many hacks. A starting point for finding an adviser is by dialing the phone. The following associations provide information on finding an investment adviser and may even refer you to advisers near you:

- International Association for Financial Planning (800-945-4237)

- National Association of Personal Financial Advisors (888-333-6659)

- Institute of Certified Financial Planners (888-237-6275)

- LINC Society for CPA Financial Planners (800-737-2727)

Mind you, these associations should be regarded as starting points and not the final stop on your search.

Another source for candidates are trusted friends, family members, or business associates who may be able to endorse a particular adviser.

Once you have a pool of potential candidates, the next step is to interview each prospect. Questions you should ask include:

- *What are your credentials?* Ask to see the adviser's Form ADV part II, which will show business history, regulatory sanctions, criminal records, and so on.

- *How much money do you have under management?* Be careful how you evaluate this response. While someone with assets under management of less than a few million dollars may be too green for your liking, an adviser with hundreds of millions of dollars under management may not provide the attention you desire.

- *What has been your performance?* Beware of big promises that cannot be confirmed. Consider only audited financial performance. Beware of the use of "model portfolios" to show performance. Even if a model portfolio has been audited, the fact that the manager did not have real money on the line is significant. He or she may behave much differently when real dollars are at risk.

- *How do you make your money?* Many financial planners make their money from the commissions on the investments they sell you. I've never been a big fan of this way of doing business, since the adviser may be getting you into investments that carry the biggest sales fees. Preference financial advisers who receive a fee based on the value of your assets.

- *Where do you invest your own money?* I think it's useful to know if an adviser is putting his or her own money in the same investments being recommended to you.

These are just a few of the questions to ask, and I'm sure many more will come to your mind. Ask them.

REMEMBER: *This person has your financial future in his or her hands. Don't be shy.*

STREET-NAME OWNERSHIP

Brokers like you to hold stock in street name, since it limits your portability.

You might be surprised to learn that, in many instances, a company in which you hold stock doesn't even know that you are a shareholder. That's because the shares are held in street name—in other words, in the name of the broker.

When investors buy stock, they can have the shares registered in one of two ways—in street name (the name of the brokerage firm doing the trade) or in the name of the shareholder. When shares are held in street name, all correspondence between the company and the investor goes through the brokerage firm. Interestingly, the company usually does not even have the investor's name.

Most investors aren't even aware of the distinction. That's not surprising, since most brokerage firms herd investors into street-name ownership and never push registering the stock in the name of the investor. The reason that brokers like their customers to hold stock in street name is that the broker, in effect, controls the assets.

There are advantages to owning stock in street name, such as having all your holdings displayed on a consolidated brokerage statement. Having shares held at the broker relieves you of holding stock certificates in a safety deposit box.

Nevertheless, when you hold stock in street name, you pay the price in reduced freedom to shop around for brokers when it comes time to sell. Portability of shares is reduced when shares are held in street name. In addition, most company-sponsored dividend reinvestment plans—plans which allow shareholders to buy stock directly from the companies—don't permit street-name investors to participate. Thus, by holding stock in street name, you eliminate yourself from perhaps the best investing avenue for the small investor.

DIRECT REGISTRATION

There is a movement away from stock certificates to an electronic registration, book-entry form of ownership.

If you're a shareholder in AT&T, you've seen what the future holds for stock certificates.

When AT&T spun off its NCR unit to shareholders, AT&T shareholders received one share of NCR stock for every 16 shares of AT&T held. AT&T shareholders with fewer than 16 shares received a cash payment instead of a fractional share. Since spinning off companies has become commonplace in corporate America in recent years, what AT&T did with its NCR unit is hardly unique, right?

Guess again.

What's unique about the NCR spin-off was how NCR's new shares were distributed to registered shareholders. Under the old way of distributing shares in spin-offs, registered shareholders in AT&T would have received stock certificates for the new shares in NCR. For the NCR spin-off, however, no physical "shares" of NCR were sent to registered shareholders. The NCR shares were issued in electronic registration form. Instead of receiving stock certificates, investors received an account statement showing the number of full and fractional shares registered with NCR.

There is a movement in the U.S. equities markets away from stock certificates to an electronic registration, book-entry form of securities ownership. One reason is that electronic registration is less costly to issuing companies. Also, some market regulators believe that physical certificates slow the trade settlement process. For individual investors, electronic registration eliminates the risk of stock certificates being lost, stolen, or damaged.

The NCR spin-off is only one of the first manifestations of this move toward a "certificate-less" stock market. In November 1996, a pilot "direct registration system" began. The direct registration system is a form of electronic registration whereby investors who want to be registered directly with the corporation have the option of receiving account statements rather than a physical certificate. The direct registration system has been championed by the Securities and Exchange Commission as a way to provide registration choices that are more convenient for investors, less costly for corporations, and more efficient for trade settlement.

Will a direct registration system make stock certificates go the way of the buggy whip? Perhaps, but it may take several more years before stock certificates are a thing of the past. Under the pilot direct registration system (and with the NCR spin-off, too), investors still have the option of receiving physical certificates if they desire.

ON-LINE TRADING

While trading on-line via the computer may be convenient, it's far from trouble-free.

America Online, the leading on-line service, makes headlines periodically when its system goes down. Such crashes cause the millions of AOL subscribers to be unable to access their e-mail or to access AOL sites.

I bring this up not so much for how it relates to America Online as how it relates to the on-line world in general and on-line trading systems in particular. One of the growing trends in the brokerage industry is to allow investors to enter trades on-line, via the computer. Obviously, such trading has its advantages in terms of ease and convenience.

However, there is a downside to trading mechanisms that depend on computer technology—they don't always work. During busy market days, a number of on-line traders have complained that they were unable to execute a trade in a timely fashion. Of course, busy market days may make it difficult to conduct business via the telephone as well—witness what happened during the market crash of 1987, when many investors got busy signals when calling their brokers.

Another aspect of on-line investing is that the security of the transaction, while improving, still does not match the security of doing business over the telephone on a recorded line.

Over time, of course, the kinks in the system will be worked out, and on-line trading will probably be the way most trades are conducted. But for now, investors should approach such trading systems with a healthy cautiousness, realizing that the systems may not be trouble-free.

CHILDREN AND INVESTMENTS

Be careful how you set up an investment account for your kindergarten capitalist.

A big business these days is educating children about stocks and personal finance. There are summer investing camps for kids ("Dear Mom: Send bug spray and my Value Line"). There are books focused on kids and investing. There's even a mutual fund (Stein Roe Young Investor Fund—800-338-2550) marketed to kids that invests in kid-friendly firms.

I think introducing children to the investing game at an early age is a good idea, and I'm sure you do, too. After all, the sooner Biff or Buffie understands the importance of investing and savings, the sooner he or she has seven figures in the bank and can take care of dear old mom and dad, right?

Before your kindergarten capitalist becomes the next Warren Buffett, he or she will need to open an account, at either a mutual fund, or a brokerage firm, or perhaps in a company's dividend reinvestment plan. When establishing an account for a child, consider the following factors:

- A common account registration for a child is called a Uniform Gift to Minor's Account, otherwise known as a UGMA. In a UGMA, the account is registered in the name of the child, and a custodian (most likely a parent or grandparent) is assigned to the account. The benefit of a UGMA is that taxes on the account are paid at the child's tax rate, which is likely to be much lower than the parent's rate. The downside is that control of the account's assets reverts to the child when he or she reaches the age of majority, which is 18 in most states. Thus, if Buffie decides to run off with Snake the biker when she hits age 18, she can empty her account and do with it as she pleases. Another potential downside to a UGMA is that Biff may have trouble securing college financial aid if he has a big chunk of money in the UGMA. In making financial aid decisions, colleges look closely at how much children can contribute to their college education and would view big assets in a UGMA as dollars earmarked for college.

- Another way to invest for a child is merely to open an account in the parent's or grandparent's name and earmark the funds for the child at some point down the road. The upside is that the adult maintains control of the account for as long as desired. The downside is that the adult is responsible for the taxes.

Other possible avenues include trusts that can be established on the child's behalf. Such trusts are best established with the help of an expert in that field. When implementing an investment program for a child, consult with all the parties to make sure the account is established in a way that eliminates surprises down the road.

MY BROKER, MY MORTGAGE COMPANY

If your parents or grandparents own stock, you might be able to use their holdings to secure money for a home mortgage.

For would-be home buyers who can't scrape enough together for a down payment, there may be another way to get into that first home.

Phone home.

Parents have often been a source of down-payment money for first-time buyers. However, maybe you don't want to bother your parents for the cash.

You should still phone home, according to Merrill Lynch.

The financial services giant offers "Parent Power," a program that provides 100 percent financing for a home if a relative puts up collateral valued at 39 percent or more of the purchase price of the home. The collateral must be in liquid securities, such as stocks, bonds, and mutual funds, but not tax-sheltered accounts, such as IRAs. The sponsor retains control over the assets and continues to receive interest and dividends.

There are certain fees attached to loans generated in this manner, and the program is not for everyone. However, if your parents or grandparents have huge stock and bond holdings, this option is something to consider.

BUYING STOCKS WITHOUT A BROKER

One way to cut out the broker is by investing via dividend reinvestment plans.

There are many myths in the stock market. One of them is that you need a broker to conduct stock transactions.

Not true.

Private stock transactions can occur between consenting parties merely by transferring ownership of securities. It may not always be easy to link a buyer and a seller. However, between family members or friends, such transactions are permissible. Of course, transactions that give extremely generous terms in order to dodge taxes may draw the ire of the IRS. Nevertheless, sales between private parties may take place.

Another way that the broker is eliminated is through direct purchase of stock from companies. Over 1,000 companies have dividend reinvestment programs (DRIPs), which permit participants who already have shares in the firms to make additional purchases without using a broker or incurring commissions. Shares are purchased in two ways:

- Instead of sending dividend checks to investors, the company reinvests the dividends to purchase additional shares.

- Most DRIPs permit optional cash investments whereby investors may send money directly to the company. In many cases, the minimum investments via optional cash payments are just $10 to $50.

In order to enroll in many DRIPs, an investor must first be a shareholder of the company. Most companies permit investors owning just one share to join the plan. In order to join a DRIP, you must have the qualifying share or shares registered in your name, not in street name.

My book *Buying Stocks Without a Broker* (McGraw-Hill) provides a comprehensive guide to DRIPs. The book is available in bookstores or by calling (800) 711-7969.

THE BUDDY SYSTEM

Your friend or relative can be the source for the one share of stock you need to join a DRIP.

One way to obtain the necessary share or shares needed to join a company's dividend reinvestment plan is by using the "buddy system." Let's say that you already own shares in Coca-Cola. You can transfer one of your shares from your account to an account set up for your "buddy" who wants to own Coca-Cola shares in order to join the dividend reinvestment plan.

Transferring shares is easy. Just secure a stock power form from a broker or the company's transfer agent. Fill out the stock power form. When you've done this, take the form to a bank to receive a "medallion" signature guarantee. Once the form has been stamped with the medallion, return it to the transfer agent. You might want to include a letter stating your intentions and specifying that you would like to enroll the individual directly in the dividend reinvestment plan. Most companies will oblige.

The transfer process costs little or no money to complete and is very easy.

NO-LOAD STOCKS™

More than 300 companies allow you to buy your first share and every share directly from the firm, without a broker.

Wouldn't it be great if you could walk into McDonald's and buy two Big Macs, two fries, and two shares of McDonald's stock? What if you could go into your local Wal-Mart and buy bug spray, a new sprinkler, and five shares of Wal-Mart stock?

Unfortunately, buying stock is not that easy. However, a growing number of companies are making stock investing a little easier by implementing no-load stock programs.

Most investors are familiar with no-load mutual funds. These are mutual funds that are bought directly from the fund group, without using a broker and paying brokerage fees. No-load stocks work under the same principle of dealing direct, without using a broker. The programs are set up to permit investors to invest directly by sending a check to the company. In most cases, the minimum investments are $250 to $500, although a few no-load stock programs can be initiated for as little as $50.

In addition to the direct purchase feature, several no-load stocks have adopted features usually associated only with mutual funds. For example, a number of no-load stock programs will allow investors to invest directly into an Individual Retirement Account established by the company. Most no-load stock programs permit automatic cash investments with electronic withdrawals from an investor's bank account.

More than 300 companies offer no-load stock plans. That number is up from just 52 at the end of 1994. Prominent companies currently offering no-load stock programs include Exxon, Merck, Gillette, McDonald's, International Business Machines, BellSouth, and Texaco. In order to enroll in a company's no-load stock plan, you must secure an enrollment form and plan prospectus from the company. Firms have toll-free numbers to handle enrollment requests. A complete list of no-load stocks and their phone numbers is available by writing *No-Load Stock Insider* newsletter, 7412 Calumet Avenue, Suite 200, Hammond, IN 46324. Also, my book *No-Load Stocks* (McGraw-Hill) provides one-page profiles on more than 145 no-load stocks. The book is available in bookstores or by calling (800) 711-7969.

FEES AND
NO-LOAD STOCKS™

Consider fees when investing in certain direct stock purchase plans.

The rapid growth in the number of no-load stocks has been accompanied by growth in the number of plans charging fees. These fees include one-time enrollment fees, annual administrative fees, and per-transaction fees. While these fees are generally still well below what an investor would pay to purchase shares through the broker, the growing use of fees adds another factor to consider when evaluating no-load stock investments.

Fortunately, many top-quality firms still provide "no fee" no-load stock plans. The following companies represent excellent choices among "no fee" no-load stocks. These issues have no enrollment fees, no annual administrative fees, and no purchase fees. (These companies may, however, charge fees to sell shares through the plans.)

- Exxon remains one of the Cadillacs among no-load stocks, and the fact that the firm offers a "no fee" plan enhances its appeal even more. These shares have shown the ability to hold up well during good and bad times in the oil sector. Minimum initial investment is $250. Subsequent investments may be made for $50 to $100,000 per year. Optional cash payments are invested weekly. Automatic monthly investment via electronic withdrawals from a bank account is available. An IRA option is available. For further information and an enrollment form, call (800) 252-1800.

- Regions Financial is a leading bank in the Southeast. Net income has risen annually for more than two decades. I view Regions as a win-win situation for investors. Steadily rising profits and dividends should help drive the stock price higher. With takeover activity likely to heat up even more in the banking field, Regions' strong market presence in a highly desirable part of the country should eventually attract a large bank wanting to expand in the Southeast. I own these shares and feel they have further upside potential. Minimum initial investment is $500. Subsequent investments may range from $25 to $120,000 per year. Optional cash payments are invested monthly. Automatic investment services are available. Shares may be sold through the plan over the telephone. For further information and an enrollment form, call (800) 922-3468.

BUYING ADRs WITHOUT A BROKER

Investors can now diversify a portfolio to include international stocks—and do so without ever calling a broker.

A n exciting development in the no-load stock world is the growth of direct purchase programs offered by

J. P. Morgan and Bank of New York. These companies are major providers of administrative services for foreign companies whose ADRs—American depositary receipts—trade in the United States. Investors buy and sell ADRs just like ordinary common shares. (See page 32 for an explanation of ADRs.)

Morgan's Shareholder Services Program permits initial purchases in a growing number of foreign companies, including such household names as Sony, British Airways, Reuters Holdings, and Royal Dutch Petroleum. Minimum initial investment in Morgan's plan is $250.

Bank of New York's Global BuyDIRECT plan permits minimum initial investments of $200 in such foreign companies as Vodafone Group, Beecham Smithkline, and Luxottica Group.

The advent of ADRs offering no-load stock plans is significant in that investors can now diversify no-load stock investments internationally. For further information and enrollment forms for companies participating in Morgan's ADR direct purchase plan, call (800) 749-1687. For information and enrollment forms for Bank of New York's Global BuyDIRECT plan, call (800) 345-1612.

ONE-STOP SHOPPING FOR NO-LOAD STOCKS™

The Direct Stock Purchase Plan Clearinghouse offers one-stop shopping for no-load stock enrollment information.

If you want to know how to get started investing in a no-load stock, the first step is to find out which companies offer the programs. Unfortunately, the Securities and Exchange Commission has restrictions on a company's ability to get the word out about its no-load stock plan. And even if you know a company has a plan, you still need to know the toll-free number to call to request the enrollment information.

In order to assist investors in enrolling in no-load stock plans, my firm, in conjunction with New York-based Shareholder Communications Corp., has established the Direct Stock Purchase Plan Clearinghouse. The clearinghouse provides a one-stop shop for investors who want the necessary enrollment information to join a growing number of direct stock purchase plans. To use the free service, investors should call the 24-hour clearinghouse hotline number—(800) 774-4117. The toll-free call connects to an automated system that permits investors to request the necessary enrollment and prospectus information to get started investing in a host of no-load stocks.

REMEMBER: The call is free for investors. The costs of the clearinghouse are shouldered by participating companies.

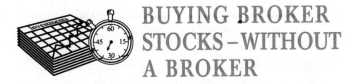

BUYING BROKER STOCKS – WITHOUT A BROKER

You don't need a broker to buy Charles Schwab stock.

W ant to know how to drive a Charles Schwab broker crazy? Mention that you can buy the company's stock without a broker and without paying any commission.

One of the great ironies in the world of investments is that Charles Schwab offers a company-sponsored dividend reinvestment plan. Participants in Schwab's DRIP may make optional cash investments of up to $5,000 per month, commission-free, to purchase Schwab stock. Investors must own at least one share of Schwab stock in order to enroll in the dividend reinvestment plan. For further information on the Schwab plan, call the company's transfer agent, Norwest, at (800) 670-4763.

POCKET CHANGE PORTFOLIO

With just $50, you can invest in top-quality companies directly and pay little or no fees.

W hat can you do with $50? Take the family to the movies? Enjoy dinner for two at a fancy-but-not-too-fancy restaurant?

How about buying some stock?

Indeed, with just $50, you can take initial positions directly in any one of the following companies:

- Johnson Controls (call 800-524-6220 to receive a prospectus and plan enrollment form) provides building-control systems and automotive components. The stock has given a good account of itself in recent years and has favorable upside potential.

- Bob Evans Farms (800-272-7675) operates a restaurant chain. A renewed focus on its core restaurant business and ample geographic expansion opportunities should help these low-priced shares rebound.

- For utility investors, two quality Wisconsin-based utilities—Madison Gas & Electric (800-356-6423) and Wisconsin Energy (800-558-9663)—may be purchased directly with just $50.

DRIPs IN CYBERSPACE

You'll see more companies taking advantage of the Internet to sell shares directly to investors.

It was only a matter of time before some enterprising young company decided to use cyberspace to bypass Wall Street. The company, Spring Street Brewing, broke new ground when it offered a bulletin board stock trading system on its World Wide Web home page. The board allows buyers and sellers of Spring Street Brewing to meet via e-mail. If the buyers and sellers agree to a deal, Spring Street provides an agreement-and-acceptance form that parties can complete by e-mail, fax, or mail. Spring Street accepts no fees for its service.

Andrew Klein, the chief executive of Spring Street Brewing, says he has taken calls and received letters from numerous companies about his system. Klein claims that the system could be used by bigger companies.

When reading about Spring Street Brewing, I can't help but get excited about the possible marriage of dividend reinvestment plans (DRIPs) with computer technology. Buying stocks directly from companies via the Internet, receiving DRIP statements electronically, even logging into your DRIP account at a particular company via your home computer—all of this and much more will likely be available soon.

While not good news for brokers, this should put smiles on the faces of DRIP investors everywhere.

SELLING STOCKS WITHOUT A BROKER

Just as it is possible to buy stocks without a broker, so you can sell stocks without a broker under certain circumstances.

One way to sell stocks without a broker is by joining a company's dividend reinvestment plan. Most investors join a DRIP to buy stocks directly from the company. Most DRIPs also allow participants to sell shares in the plan. Some plans have telephone sale services whereby an investor can sell the shares over the phone; the sale will take place within a 24-hour period. Most DRIPs, however, require you to submit your sell instructions in writing, and the sale could take 5 to 10 business days. In short, you won't get the same execution speed you would by selling through a broker. The upside is that the costs will likely be much lower to sell via the DRIP.

Selling stock through a DRIP is especially cost-effective if you want to sell a relatively small number of shares. Many investors may find themselves holding less than a round lot (a round lot is 100 shares of a particular company) because of the large number of corporate spin-offs in recent years. Selling 5 or 10 shares through a broker is likely to cost you $20 or more. Selling 5 or 10 shares through the DRIP could cost as little as a couple of bucks. If you find yourself in the position of having just a few shares of a stock and you have no interest in adding to the position, check to see if the firm has a DRIP. This might be the cheapest way to sell the shares.

Another way to unload a few shares of stock is via an odd-lot buyback program, in which a company offers to buy back stock from investors who hold fewer than 100 shares. Companies offer buyback programs to lower their shareholder-servicing costs by eliminating small shareholders. In some cases, a company may buy the shares back without charging you a fee. More likely, however, some fee will be charged, perhaps 50 cents or 75 cents per share. If you are offered a chance to sell shares back to a company via an odd-lot buyback program—you'll be notified of such an offer by mail—make sure the fees are lower than what you'd pay selling through a broker. For example, if you have 5 or 10 shares, paying 50 cents per share is still cheaper than selling through a broker. If you have 50 shares, you might be able to get a better deal through the broker.

If you want to find out if a company of interest has an odd-lot buyback program, call its shareholder services department.

BUYING TREASURY SECURITIES WITHOUT A BROKER

A way exists to bypass commissions altogether by buying Treasury securities directly from the Federal Reserve.

With some investors seeking a safe haven for their funds because of the volatility of the stock market, Treasury securities have grown in popularity. Primary attractions of Treasury securities are their safety and salability. Interest earned from Treasury securities is exempt from state and local income taxes.

In most cases, investors pay a fee for purchasing Treasury securities through their bank or broker. However, there is a way to bypass commissions altogether.

Treasury bills are obligations issued with a term of one

year or less. Treasury notes are 1- to 10-year obligations. Treasury bonds are obligations greater than 10 years. All may be purchased directly, without a service charge, from most of the Federal Reserve banks or their branches or the U.S. Treasury Department's Bureau of the Public Debt.

Treasury securities are sold through an auction process. Individuals may submit bids at the time of the auction. Prospective purchasers merely indicate the amount of securities they wish to purchase. Treasury notes and bonds are sold in minimum denominations of $1,000 and $5,000. Treasury bills are sold in minimum amounts of $10,000. Purchasers may make a competitive bid, in which they specify the yield they are willing to accept, or a noncompetitive bid, in which they agree to accept the weighted-average yield established in the auction.

For information on purchasing procedures and upcoming Treasury auctions, contact a Federal Reserve bank in your region. Additional information may be obtained by reading *Buying Treasury Securities at Federal Reserve Banks*, a booklet available for $4.50 (send a check) from the Federal Reserve Bank of Richmond, Public Services Department, P.O. Box 27471, Richmond, VA 23261.

5
INVESTMENT TOOLS AND INDICATORS

If nothing else, the future promises to be more confusing for investors. We'll be faced with unprecedented financial choices during a time when market volatility will likely be escalating. Such complex and uncertain times call for simple, time-tested investment tools. This chapter provides a number of user-friendly investment tools and indicators for picking stocks, assessing overall market risk, determining the market's primary trend, and forecasting interest rates.

LOOK AT YOUR INVESTMENT ALTERNATIVES

If yields on certificates of deposit and money-market accounts are low, chances are investors won't be selling stocks.

D epending on to whom you talk, there are always plenty of reasons to be bearish or bullish about the stock market. The plethora of technical indicators, fundamental data, computer-aided research, and other tools, can literally drown an investor in confusion. However, one quick analysis that an investor can make to judge the soundness of holding stocks is this: "What are my alternatives, and are they as attractive as stocks?"

For example, if stocks seem high, but the yields on money markets and CDs are only 3 percent or 4 percent, it is not likely that investors will be doing wholesale selling of stocks. The alternative investments are just not that attractive. On the other hand, if bonds and fixed-income investments are providing yields of 8 percent or more, competition with stocks heightens and the chances for a pullback in the market rise.

THE DOW THEORY

The fact that the Dow Theory has stood the test of time gives credence to its ability to forecast market turns.

Readers of the financial pages have no doubt seen mention of the venerable Dow Theory, but just what is this market forecasting tool?

The Dow Theory, developed before the turn of the century by Charles H. Dow, first publisher of *The Wall Street Journal*, looks at the movement of the Dow Jones Industrial Average and Dow Jones Transportation Average.

In a nutshell, the Dow Theory states that these averages reflect at any given time all that is known and all that can be foreseen by financial and lay minds concerning financial matters. With that premise, the Dow Theory states that any market signal, in order to be authentic, must be confirmed by both the Industrial and Transportation Averages. This tenet of confirmation is key in understanding the Dow Theory. Confirmation by the averages, either to new highs or to new lows, is a sign that the trend is in place.

When the averages are not in unison, such as one average moving to a new high while the other one lags, it is a time for caution. The Dow Theory states that the only trend that matters is the market's "primary trend," which generally lasts 18 months or longer. Day-to-day market movements offer little forecasting value and should be ignored in most cases.

Because major bullish or bearish signals under the Dow Theory last for several months—and, indeed, years (the Dow Theory pegs the current bull market as having begun in January 1991)—users of the theory do not find themselves being "whipsawed" by short-term market developments—bullish today, bearish tomorrow, bullish again two weeks later, and so on. Timing tools that focus on short-term market movements leave their users vulnerable to missing big market advances. Also, short-term timing tools, because they call for buying and selling stocks on a much more frequent basis than the Dow Theory, cause their users to rack up painful transaction fees.

While no market timing tool is infallible, the Dow Theory's record through the years has been impressive and is one reason this market tool has stood the test of time.

USING THE DOW JONES INDUSTRIAL YIELD AS A MARKET INDICATOR

When using the Dow's yield as a market indicator, be sure to consider the prevailing income tax rate.

One financial-services firm's motto reminds investors that it's not what you earn that matters, it's what you keep.

This point is especially important when evaluating the stock market on the basis of the historical yield on the Dow Jones Industrial Average. Many investors make the case that, with a Dow Jones Industrial yield of 3 percent or less, stocks are richly valued, since this level is well below historical ranges.

However, investors often fail to take into account prevailing income tax rates. At one time, the top tax bracket was 70 percent. Today, the top tax bracket is considerably lower. With a lower tax bracket, investors keep more of their dividend income. That is why you must figure the current yield on the market in light of the tax brackets. With a 3 percent yield, the after-tax equivalent is a higher yield when you take into account a previous 50 percent or 70 percent top tax bracket.

That's not to say that the market is cheap when it yields around 3 percent, only that it may not be as overvalued as some investors believe.

TECHNICAL ANALYSIS

Technicians believe that everything that can be known about a company is reflected in the stock price.

There are generally two schools of thought on stock analysis. One school, which is arguably the more popular, is fundamental analysis. Advocates of fundamental analysis examine such factors as a company's earnings, financial strength, and industry trends. The major goal of fundamental analysis is to discern a company's intrinsic value relative to the stock price.

Technicians, on the other hand, believe that everything that can be known about a company and its stock is already reflected in the stock price. A big part of technical analysis predicts future stock price action from past stock market patterns. One popular tool used for forecasting is a head-and-shoulders formation. This stock chart pattern, which resembles a human head and shoulders, is generally negative for stock prices.

Another popular technical strategy is to compare the stock's price with its 200-day moving average. The thinking behind this tool is that a stock price generally returns to its long-run average price. A stock that is trading well above its 200-day moving average can be expected to decline to the average. Likewise, a stock trading below its 200-day moving average can be expected to move upward toward the average.

Other tools used by technicians include the ratio of put to call option purchases, the number of stocks making new highs versus those making new lows, and various volume indicators.

The fact that many investors use technical analysis lends some credibility to the method, though most academicians believe that technical analysis has little forecasting ability. My feeling is that picking stocks is just as much art as it is science, and there are useful tools from both technical and fundamental analysis that can be employed in a profitable investment strategy.

MEASURING INVESTOR SENTIMENT

Explosion in the new-issues market is a sign that stocks may be ready to correct.

Getting a real handle on the amount of bullishness or bearishness in the market is akin to grabbing at shadows. Many analysts talk out of both sides of their mouths, thus affording little insight into what investors and Wall Street are truly thinking about the market. However, there are some telltale signs that the stock market has become overly bullish and is ripe for a correction:

- Explosion in the new-issues market. A strong stock market usually brings out a plethora of companies that want to go public to take advantage of investors' new-found love of stocks.

- Price surges in penny stocks and other extremely speculative issues. This is a strong indication of an overvalued market.

- An increased number of companies taking advantage of higher stock prices by issuing additional stock.

SHORT INTEREST

A high short-interest reading is usually considered bullish.

O ne way to tap into what investors are thinking is by examining the short-interest readings reported regularly in *The Wall Street Journal.* A short sale is the sale of borrowed stock by an investor who hopes to buy back the stock at a lower price, thus making a profit. Short sellers are betting on a drop in the market and are bearish. Short interest is the number of shares that will eventually have to be bought back by short sellers.

What does all this mean for the market?

Interestingly, a high short-interest reading is generally considered bullish. That's because the borrowed shares must eventually be repurchased by investors, thus providing buying power to the market.

ASSESSING MARKET RISK

When less than 40 percent of New York Stock Exchange stocks are trading above their 200-day moving averages, intermediate risk is low in the market.

W hile I acknowledge that it is extremely difficult to time the market successfully, I do believe there are helpful tools in giving investors a snapshot of where the market stands in terms of risk. One of the most useful tools for determining intermediate market risk uses the percentage of stocks on the New York Stock Exchange trading above their 200-day moving averages. This information is provided daily in *Investor's Business Daily* newspaper.

In a nutshell, when less than 40 percent of stocks on the New York Stock Exchange are trading above their 200-day moving averages, I consider the market's intermediate trend to be in low-risk territory. I consider neutral territory to be any time the percentage is between 40 percent and 70 percent. When 70 percent of the stocks on the New York Stock Exchange are trading above their 200-day moving averages, the market's intermediate-term risk level is high.

Why does using the percentage of stocks trading above their 200-day moving averages seem to work so well? One reason is that this indicator provides a useful gauge for assessing stocks' popularity. The best time to buy stocks is when they are least popular. If the majority of stocks trade below their 200-day moving average, it reflects a market in which most investors are rather bearish. Conversely, a market in which most stocks trade above their 200-day moving averages reflects a market in which stocks are richly valued.

PRICE-SALES RATIOS (PSRs)

PSRs offer an excellent yardstick for determining a stock's value.

Spotting value is a major key to success in the stock market. There are a number of yardsticks which analysts use to determine value: a stock's book value, a stock's price-earnings ratio, or the company's liquidation value. Another way to measure value is by examining a company's price-sales ratio (PSR).

To compute a PSR, take the company's stock price and multiply it by the number of outstanding shares. This figure is the firm's market capitalization. It represents, in effect, how much Wall Street is valuing the company. When you have this figure, divide it by the company's annual sales. The result is the PSR. For example, a company with a market capitalization of $500 million and annual sales of $1 billion has a PSR of 0.5.

Generally speaking, a PSR value of 1 or below indicates that investors are not richly valuing the company. Low PSRs may be due to a number of factors, including low profit margins and poor profitability.

However, an issue with a low PSR has the opportunity for big gains in the event that it can begin to generate greater profits from its sales base.

Just because a stock has a low PSR doesn't make it a good value. However, it does earmark certain firms for closer inspection.

A MARKET OF STOCKS

Examining a company in terms of its total market value can be enlightening.

Sometimes it's best to evaluate stocks by looking at what the company is worth in the market in total, not on a per-share basis.

When one stock is compared to another, it may be difficult to get a real handle on which seems cheap and which seems dear. However, by looking at the total value that Wall Street is assigning the two companies (their market capitalizations), you can often get a different perspective.

For example, at the time of this writing, the market value of Microsoft exceeds $152 billion. It's hard to get a handle on exactly what that means, but comparisons may help. Indeed, the market is valuing Microsoft nearly as much as it values the entire U.S. auto industry (Ford, Chrysler, General Motors) plus the U.S. airline industry (AMR, Delta, UAL, Southwest Airlines, US Airways Group) plus McDonald's. Is Microsoft really worth the same as these companies combined? Or is the stock dramatically overvalued? Only time will tell. Still, examining a company in these terms may provide a helpful perspective in valuing a company.

THE "ONE"
INDICATOR

When investing in a particular industry, make sure you understand the "one" success factor for that group.

W hen an investor evaluates stocks in certain industries, it's especially important to understand what
the one biggest success factor is for that industry.

For example, when looking at retailing stocks, don't be
fooled by a company whose sales are growing rapidly
primarily because of store expansion. The figure that
truly counts is what "same-store sales" are doing. Same-
store sales figures compare a store's sales this period with
the year-earlier period. Same-store sales are important,
since that figure gives a clearer picture of whether the
company's growth is coming from real revenue growth at
each of its outlets or merely growth resulting from a larger number of outlets (growth that is not likely to be sustainable over time).

The "one" indicator when evaluating utility stocks is
the utility's cost per unit of electricity. This figure is
found in the utility's annual report. Low-cost utilities are
in a much better position to compete in the new world of
utility competition than utilities with high costs. Low-
cost utilities usually have stronger financial positions,
which means better-than-average dividend growth.

Of course, other factors will influence the performance of retailers and utilities. However, without good
numbers in the "one" area, it is unlikely that a particular

retailer or utility will provide above-average returns for investors.

Before investing in any particular industry sector, be sure you understand the "one" success indicator for that industry group.

HOW TO READ MARKET VOLUME

What you like to see during bull markets is volume rising on up days and declining on down days.

Wall Streeters have many strategies for using market volume as a tool for discerning market trend. The problem lies, however, in determining what is "heavy" volume versus "light" volume.

I can remember when I first started in this business in 1982. It was rather unusual to see trading days of 100 million shares. Today, trading volume of 300 million is considered extremely light.

Because of the changing scale denoting heavy and light volume, the best way to look at daily trading volume is on a relative, not an absolute, basis. I use market volume primarily to confirm the market's primary trend. As a rule, volume follows the market's trend. Ideally, what you like to see during bull markets is market volume rising on up days and declining on down days. Conversely, a downward market trend will likely continue if you see market volume swell on down days and decline on up days.

Volume can often be a helpful tool in determining a change in market trend. A tiring bull market will begin to see volume declining on up days and expanding on down days. Conversely, a bear market may be nearing its end if volume starts to decline on down days and build on rallies.

PORTFOLIO INSURANCE

Put options can limit downside risk, but this insurance comes with a price.

Portfolio insurance is a strategy by which institutional investors protect their portfolios by buying insurance in the form of options and futures that kick in during market declines. These options and futures produce profits during a time when the portfolio's value is dropping, thus offsetting the loss.

Individual investors are not excluded from owning portfolio insurance. The options market is a good place to start in developing strategies for portfolio insurance. One insurance policy is a put option. Put options give investors the right to sell stock at a given price. Investors usually buy put options on stocks that they believe will drop in value. As the stock price declines, the put option increases in value.

In addition to speculating in puts, many investors use

them to hedge their portfolios. In this scenario, investors buy put options on stocks they hold in their portfolios if they think the market is going to correct. If they're right, the stocks in the portfolio will decline in value, but the options will rise in value, thus offsetting some of the losses.

Remember that put options, like any insurance, cost money to purchase. Thus, investors have to weigh the pros and cons of being insured.

Another strategy investors use is to sell call options on stocks they hold. A call option gives the holder the option of buying a stock at a set price. The option seller receives a premium when selling a call, which reduces the downside risk in the underlying stock by the amount of the premium that the seller receives. However, the risk in selling call options is that an investor's stock, should it reach the strike price of the call option, could be "called away." In other words, the holder of the call option may exercise the option and buy the stock from the seller of the call, in which case the investor would be forced to sell the issue unless he or she buys back the call option at the higher price.

As you can see, selling calls has its own set of risks. However, if you are concerned that your stock holdings will decline, selling calls provides a way to build an income stream that can help offset some of the price drops in your stocks.

TRACKING CORPORATE INSIDERS

A corporate insider who buys company stock is likely feeling optimistic about the firm's prospects.

One of the better ways to track stocks, in my opinion, is by seeing what insiders are doing. By insiders, I mean corporate executives and directors, supposedly the individuals in the know.

It is legal for top corporate management and directors to buy or sell shares in their own companies. They must, however, report the trades to the Securities and Exchange Commission. This information is available to the public and provided in a number of financial publications, including *Barron's* and *The Wall Street Journal* (every Wednesday).

I think it is more significant when insiders buy stock than when they sell. Insiders may have many reasons to sell stock that are unrelated to the company's prospects— college tuition, portfolio diversification, holiday gifts. However, a corporate insider who buys company stock is likely feeling optimistic about the company's prospects and believes the stock is undervalued.

Investors should note that insiders are often early in their buying; it is not unusual for insiders to buy a stock that remains in the doldrums for a few months. However, over time I think that insiders have pretty good instincts concerning their companies, so it makes sense to follow their lead, especially if insiders are investing in stocks that have undergone substantial declines and are now poised to rebound.

JANUARY EFFECT

Small-capitalization stocks tend to outperform bigger stocks in the month of January.

The January effect occurs when small-capitalization and secondary stocks outperform large, blue chips in the month of January.

One reason given for this seasonal market tendency is that small-capitalization stocks are hit hard with tax-loss selling toward the end of the year, since these issues are predominantly owned by individuals. With most of the selling purged in December, any buying in January drives their stock prices higher.

Another reason is that professional money managers who have done well during the year may lock up their gains—and their bonuses for beating the market—by selling more risky secondary issues in December. Then, in January, these money managers return to secondary issues, thereby driving the stock prices higher.

A third reason that may positively influence the January effect occurs when small-capitalization stocks have underperformed the market. At that time, small-cap stocks probably have better risk-reward ratios than the large-capitalization stocks that led the market.

Keep in mind that not all small-cap stocks will benefit from the January effect. Investors should focus on small-caps with strong earnings growth, solid financial positions, and the ability to generate investor interest.

JANUARY BELLWETHER

Many investors believe that market strength in January means market strength for the year overall.

How important is the market's performance in January? According to many market watchers, how the stock market performs in the first week of January and for the month overall dictates the market's performance for the remainder of the year.

There is some history to support this notion. However, as is the case with any forecasting tool, it's not perfect. We need go back only to 1994 to see an exception to the theory. Indeed, the Dow Jones Industrial Average rose more than 5 percent in January 1994, with the Dow Industrials peaking on January 31. However, over the course of the rest of the year, the Dow Industrials fell, with the Industrial Average showing only a 2 percent gain for 1994 overall.

REMEMBER: *When analysts cite seasonal market tendencies, it doesn't necessarily mean that these tendencies always hold up. It's always better to base investment decisions on fundamental notions of value than to buy or sell on the basis of historical trading patterns.*

PREDICTING INTEREST RATES

The Dow Jones Utility Average is an excellent barometer of future interest-rate direction.

Predicting interest rates can be a losing proposition—just ask any economist. Nevertheless, there is one barometer of future interest-rate direction that has an enviable record, and it is available for the price of a newspaper.

The Dow Jones Utility Average has a good track record of forecasting interest rates. Electric utilities are sensitive to interest-rate movements in a number of ways. Since utilities are capital intensive, they are susceptible to movements in the cost of funds. Also, utilities are often regarded as income investments. Therefore, when interest rates rise, alternative investments, such as money-market funds, will become more attractive.

That is why the Dow Jones Utility Average, which consists of 15 widely held utilities, will generally act poorly during a climate of rising interest rates, and vice versa.

Investors who want to monitor the action of the Dow Jones Utility Average can find a chart of the average every day in *The Wall Street Journal*.

DON'T WASTE YOUR TIME

Don't waste your time "Fed watching."

Y ou're too busy to spend time on things that don't matter. Unfortunately, many investors waste time and energy focusing on news, economic data, and other items that have no bearing on portfolio performance over time.

One of my favorite time wasters is "Fed watching." Judging from the huge number of Wall Street analysts who hang on every word coming out of the Federal Reserve Board, you'd think a separate Audubon Society had been established for watchers of the "Balded Greenspan."

Yes, I know the Fed is important, especially when it comes to interest rates. And yes, if you could discern ahead of time what the Fed was going to do with interest rates, you might have some advantage in the market. The fact is, however, that Fed chairman Alan Greenspan is so gifted at "Fedspeak"—the art of saying a lot without saying anything of substance—that studying Greenspan's words for clues about interest-rate direction is akin to studying the script of Tom Cruise's *Mission Impossible* for clues as to what the plot was all about. (One Washington wit stated that the reason it took Greenspan so long to marry longtime companion Andrea Mitchell, the Washington correspondent, was that it took Ms. Mitchell all those years to figure out that Mr. Greenspan was proposing.)

The following are actual minutes from a 1995 Fed open market committee meeting:

Accordingly, the directive stated that in the context of the Committee's long-run objectives for price stability and sustainable economic growth . . . somewhat greater reserve restraint would be acceptable or slightly lesser reserve restraint might be acceptable during the inter-meeting period.

Huh? If I'm not mistaken, doesn't that statement say that Fed tightening or loosening might be acceptable? What am I supposed to learn from that?

If you want to know where interest rates are heading, watch the Dow Jones Utility Average.

Don't waste your time trying to read the Fed's tea leaves.

INVERTED YIELD CURVES AND THE ECONOMY

Usually, an inverted yield curve precedes a downturn in the economy by about one year.

Interest rates are an important factor in stock prices. Thus, analysts watch the movement of both short-term and long-term rates very closely. An event that happens occasionally in the interest-rate market is an inverted yield curve.

Traditionally, the longer the maturity on a fixed-income investment, such as a corporate bond or Treasury bill, the higher the yield. This is because investors have to be compensated for locking up their money for a longer period of time. Under most circumstances, the yield curve rises in line with lengthening maturities.

The relationship between interest rates and maturities, however, gets inverted periodically, meaning that short-term bonds provide higher yields than long-term bonds. Inversion may happen during times when investors fear that inflation is rising.

What does all this mean for the financial markets? Usually, an inverted yield curve precedes a downturn in the economy by about one year. Some analysts feel that the growing globalization of financial markets has limited the adverse impact of an inverted yield curve. Nevertheless, it is tough to ignore the track record of inverted yield curves, which makes the relationship between short-term and long-term rates worth watching for individual investors.

USING CASH RESERVES AS A MARKET INDICATOR

Depending on how they're used, cash reserves can be a deceiving indicator.

One common indicator which investors like to use to judge whether a market has ample buying power is cash reserves in mutual funds. If cash reserves are high, the thinking is that there is plenty of buying power on the sidelines that can drive the market higher. Conversely, if cash levels are low, it generally means that all the buying has been done, and stocks are probably near the peak.

Intuitively, this indicator makes sense and has some merit as one input in determining the market trend. However, cash reserves can also be a somewhat deceiving indicator. In most cases cash reserves are expressed as a percentage of portfolio assets. If a portfolio manager has $5 million under management, $1 million in cash would be a 20 percent cash reserve.

What makes this a bit deceiving is when stock prices rise or fall. Using our previous example, say the portfolio value has now risen to $6 million because of a rise in stock prices. The firm's cash position of $1 million is now only 16 percent of the portfolio, rather than 20 percent. Keep in mind, however, that the fund manager still has the same amount in cash—$1 million.

As is the case with any indicator, cash reserves are best used in conjunction with other factors.

WHERE DO I FIND IT? TRY *THE WALL STREET JOURNAL*

The Wall Street Journal is a one-stop source for a lot of stock information.

I receive calls and letters from investors wanting to know where to find certain pieces of data about companies and the stock market. Fortunately, the best source for a lot of investor information is the daily *Wall Street Journal.*

While newcomers to investing may be intimidated by this newspaper, it truly is user-friendly and extremely accessible to even beginner investors. A big benefit of *The Wall Street Journal* is the plethora of information and data the newspaper provides on individual companies as well as the market. For example:

- *Where can I find a stock's symbol?* Stock symbols for all companies are listed next to the company's name in the *Journal*'s stock quote pages. The stock quote pages usually begin on page C3.

- *How can I find how much my company pays each year in dividends?* Company dividend information is listed in the stock quote pages for each company. The information that is listed takes the most recent quarterly dividend and annualizes that number to show how much one share of stock would receive in dividends per year.

- *What are the components of the Dow Jones Industrial Average? Dow Transportation Average? Dow Utility Average?* Down the left-hand side of page C3, the *Journal* shows the performance of the three Dow Averages. Inside the charts of the averages are small boxes containing the components for each of the averages.

- *How high or low has the stock traded over the last year?* Each stock quote listing contains the high and low price for the stock over the preceding 52 weeks.

Of course, the *Journal* contains a wealth of other information—news of daily dividends and stock splits, corporate insider buying activity, bond prices, and so on—that may be of interest to more sophisticated investors. But even beginners should get plenty out of reading this fine publication.

For my money (newsstand price of the *Journal* is 75 cents), it's the best newspaper in the United States.

"PLAIN ENGLISH" PROSPECTUS

A prospectus has a wealth of useful information for investors.

If the word "prospectus" sends chills up and down your spine, take heart.

"Plain English" is coming to the financial world.

A company issues a prospectus as part of financial documents related to stock and bond issuances and other capital-raising programs. Prospectuses are extremely useful investment tools, since they provide insight into the company's finances and management. Unfortunately, many individual investors shy away from reading them because of a perception that prospectuses are difficult for the average investor to understand.

No doubt reacting to years of investors' complaints that reading a financial prospectus required a law degree, the SEC has made a push to make prospectuses more reader-friendly. This push for "plain English" has already had its effects in the world of direct stock purchase plans—programs in which investors can buy their first share and every subsequent share directly from the company, without a broker.

BellSouth, a regional Bell company, implemented a direct stock purchase plan in 1997. The firm's prospectus explaining its plan is the first ever "plain English" prospectus for a company of its size. The prospectus, submitted under a pilot program of the SEC, provides details of the plan's features in a way that avoids all legal jargon.

I've read the plan prospectus and found it concise yet extremely informative. Furthermore, it is written in a way that even a novice investor can understand.

That BellSouth stepped up to be a pioneer for "plain English" indicates the firm's focus on reaching the individual investor. Interestingly, it seems that the individual investor has suddenly become a hot commodity. Corporations want the "little guys" among their shareholder ranks, since these individuals tend to be loyal, long-term investors, not to mention potential consumers of companies' goods and services.

Since it's a whole lot easier to woo the "little guy" if you're speaking in "plain English," expect to see many more companies follow the lead of BellSouth.

SURF'S UP

The web is merely a giant library-at-your-fingertips—not the holy grail for picking winning stocks.

If you think the World Wide Web is something that develops in the corner of your ceiling when your cleaning lady is out for six months with phlebitis, then this article is for you.

The World Wide Web (or "web," as it is called) and the Internet have apparently taken over the world. If the media are to be believed, it's now impossible to drive your car, brush your teeth, pad your expense account, or kick the cat without first going "on-line" to "surf" the web to see what the rest of "cyberspace" has to say about that particular subject.

One of the subjects that is discussed quite frequently on the Internet is investing.

I admit that I do my share of surfing the web to find interesting investment sites. I even have my own web sites (**www.dripinvestor.com** and **www.noloadstocks.com**) where I share my views with cyberinvestors. Other sites I often check out include the *Motley Fool* (**www.fool.com**), an irreverent site devoted to personal finance and investing; and *invest-o-rama* (**www.investorama.com**), a compilation of investing and personal finance sites on the web.

If you feel more like road kill on the information highway than a savvy "net" investor, take heart. It is becoming increasingly cheap and easy to access and use the Internet. Many Internet service providers—these are the firms that provide you access to the Internet—provide unlimited usage for approximately $20 a month. And computers and modems (devices that hook your computer to the Internet via a telephone line) are getting cheaper almost daily. More important, useful investment content on the web is growing, which means your ability to access market intelligence (much of it free) will only increase over time.

Remember, however, that the web is only a giant library-at-your-fingertips. That's it. It's not a surefire way to pick winning stocks. In fact, if you follow some of the garbage on the web that passes for stock advice, you may be sorry.

Use the web as a sounding board and information source—not as an investor's holy grail.

MAKE FRIENDS WITH EDGAR

The SEC's web site offers plenty of useful information.

Nowadays, a computer and a modem can take an individual investor to places he or she could never have gone in the past. One of those places is the files of the Securities and Exchange Commission.

The Securities and Exchange Commission has what I think is one of the more useful stops in cyberspace. It's the commission's site on the World Wide Web.

The SEC's web site provides the latest information and news coming from the SEC. Part of the site is a link to the Edgar electronic filing system. In Edgar, you can find a plethora of corporate filings, including quarterly and annual financial information. I have used this system to obtain information on companies and have been quite pleased with the availability of a variety of documents.

The "address" for the SEC's web site is **www.sec.gov**. I suggest you check it out.

TRACKING YOUR STOCKS WITH THE "DAILY NEWS"

An easy way exists to keep track of news on your stocks—and all it costs is a trip to the library.

Maybe you're one of those people who would like to keep better track of their stock holdings. But you don't own a computer, so you can't subscribe to any of the many computer database services available. And every time you try to call your broker to ask about some news on your stocks, she's talking with her bigger clients.

There is another way to keep up with the latest developments concerning your stocks, and all it will likely cost you is a trip to your local library. Although I don't normally plug investment products, one source of information that I find invaluable is the Standard & Poor's *Corporation Records* "Daily News" book.

This reference book contains the latest developments on literally thousands of companies. The book tracks earnings announcements, stock split news, dividend increases, management changes, corporate restructurings, stock buybacks—in short, most of the news that affects your stock holdings. The publication is updated at least once a week with news from the previous few days and is organized in a manner that makes it quick and easy to get the news on your companies.

If you have deep enough pockets, you could subscribe to the service yourself, but the price is pretty stiff ($1,465 per year). It pays to check your local library to see if it has this excellent reference source. If it doesn't, it might be worth pestering the librarian to take at least a trial subscription to the service.

Further information on the service is available at Standard & Poor's, 25 Broadway, New York, NY 10004.

6
INVESTMENT CONCEPTS AND STRATEGIES

I don't own biotechnology stocks. I don't own computer stocks. I don't own Internet stocks. I don't own robotic stocks.

I do own a hamburger maker. I do own a soft-drink company. I do own a trash hauler. I do own a drugmaker. I do own a telephone company. I do own a drugstore chain. I do own an oil company. It's human nature to overcomplicate things, including our investing methods. However, I've had the best luck staying away from things I don't understand and sticking with tried-and-true companies in industries that are easy for me to grasp.

Such a simple investment approach will not likely make me popular around the water cooler when my buddies are talking about the hot computer or biotechnology stock that's made them rich on paper. I don't worry. I've seen investors go from feast to famine in these hot stocks almost overnight. Why? Let's face it—most of us aren't smart enough to invest in such complicated industries, so none of us really knows when the worm is turning and it's time to dump the stock. Consequently, most investors are left holding the bag when hot stocks invariably disappoint Wall Street.

Do I miss opportunities for huge gains by sticking with my simple, boring investment approach? All the time. But I also don't have ulcers from seeing my stocks rise 50 percent in a month only to fall 40 percent in a day or two (any of you who have owned such wild stocks know that I'm only slightly exaggerating).

My position as editor of several investment newsletters (see the subscription information in the back of the book) gives me an excellent perch from which to view literally thousands of investors' portfolios. Three features common to the most successful portfolios are:

- Persistence
- An effective use of time
- A focus on solid, financially sound (but often boring and certainly not sexy) companies

That's why I say boring is beautiful when it comes to stocks.

This chapter explores a number of investment strategies and concepts, including the best industry groups for long-term investors, investments to avoid, and the dangers of selling stocks.

PICKING THE BEST STOCKS

Focus on companies with consistent earnings and dividend growth.

Ask 100 investors, and you'll get 100 different answers to the following question:

What are the best stocks to own?

Obviously, owning the right stocks in the right industry groups is the secret to portfolio success, and there is no holy grail for picking the right stocks for a portfolio. However, I think that profitable portfolios share a few qualities when it comes to picking the right stocks or industry groups:

- Focus on companies with consistent earnings growth. Stock prices ultimately follow earnings. While past performance is no guarantee of future results, companies that have demonstrated the ability to grow their earnings year in and year out generally are able to maintain their earnings momentum into the future.

- Focus on industry groups with steady growth prospects. I want industries whose growth prospects are better than the overall economy. That's why you don't see any cyclical companies in my portfolio.

- Focus on companies with attractive dividend growth potential. Too often, investors will look at two companies and pick the one with the highest current yield.

However, over time, dividend growth can have a huge impact on portfolio performance. For example, Philip Morris currently pays an annual dividend of $1.60 per share. A buyer of Philip Morris in 1980 now collects a yearly dividend that is greater than his or her original purchase price (adjusting for splits). If you plan to hold stocks for a long time, buy stocks whose dividends grow at a steady clip.

I WANT TO BE LIKE WARREN

Follow the master by buying the stocks he owns.

Perhaps the greatest investor of our time is Warren Buffett. In 1956 Warren, with an investment stake of $105,100 (his personal funds in the stake were the $100; family and friends accounted for the $105,000), began buying stocks for clients. Today, Warren's ownership in Berkshire Hathaway—the publicly traded company which serves as Buffett's investment vehicle—is worth approximately $20 billion.

To put this in terms that might be a little easier to grasp: If you had been one of Buffett's initial investors and given young Warren $10,000, that $10,000 would now be worth more than $183 million.

No wonder I want to be like Warren.

I also want to be like Mike—Michael Jordan, that is. However, my chances of being like Mike—I'm under six feet tall with a dismal jump shot and an hour-glass-slow first step to the hoop—are about the same as my chances of saying "I do" to Cindy Crawford.

On the other hand, I have a much better chance to be like Warren.

No, it's unlikely that I'll ever have $20 billion (if I ever do, that Cindy Crawford thing might not be such a pipe dream). But at least I can own the stocks Warren owns. How? Two ways. First, I can buy stock in Berkshire Hathaway, which trades on the New York Stock Exchange. In that way, I own exactly what Warren owns.

Unfortunately, at the time of this writing, one share of Berkshire trades for $47,000. (You read that right—a single share of Berkshire Hathaway class A stock trades for $47,000. I guess I'm not the only person who wants to be like Warren.) That's a little out of my league. Besides, I'm not so sure I'd want to invest in a stock that literally could be cut in half should Warren ever end up face down in his mashed potatoes with gravy.

Might I suggest a better way to be like Warren? Warren believes strongly in the concept of "have all your eggs in a few baskets, and watch the baskets closely." For that reason, his $20 billion fortune is spread across a surprisingly small number of stocks and investments. Simply by buying Warren's largest holdings you can be like Warren.

What does Warren own? His largest holdings are Coca-Cola, Gillette, Walt Disney, American Express, McDonald's, Washington Post, Wells Fargo, and Federal Home Loan Mortgage.

DOGS OF THE DOW

Owning the 10 highest-yielding Dow stocks has often produced superior results.

One of the more effective investment strategies over the years has been the "Dow 10" strategy, also known as the "Dogs of the Dow" strategy.

The Dow 10 strategy focuses on buying the 10 highest-yielding stocks among the 30 Dow Jones Industrial Average components. The strategy says that investors should buy the 10 highest-yielding Dow stocks at the beginning of each year, hold the portfolio for the entire year, and readjust the portfolio at the end of the year in order to hold the 10 highest-yielding stocks in the new year.

The strategy, which has done extremely well over the last 20 years, has its merits on several fronts. First, the strategy is simple and easy to follow, which is a plus for any investment strategy. A system that eliminates all emotion from the investment process is the best approach for many investors. Second, the fact that investors buy and sell shares only once a year holds down transaction costs. Third, by focusing on the highest-yielding stocks, the strategy does not rely solely on capital gains to generate performance. Also, the highest-yielding stocks tend to be those that are out of favor at that particular time. Thus, the strategy helps focus investing in stocks that may be offering the better values among the Dow stocks.

The following 10 stocks began 1997 with the highest yields among Dow components (in order of highest yield to lowest yield). Note that Texaco stock was removed from the Dow during 1997.

Philip Morris Companies	AT&T
Morgan (J. P.) & Co.	General Motors
Texaco	International Paper
Chevron	DuPont (E. I.)
Exxon	Minnesota Mining & Manufacturing

Investors should note that one potential drawback of the strategy is that investments may not be properly diversified. Indeed, among the 10 stocks for 1997, three—Chevron, Exxon, and Texaco—are pure plays in the oil sector, and a fourth, DuPont, has a sizable exposure to the oil sector via its Conoco unit. This lack of diversification increases the risks of using the strategy.

Still, investors who want a simple and time-tested way of investing their funds should at least give the Dow 10 strategy a look.

KNOW THINE INVESTMENT

It's better to invest in something you understand than to go for the "hottest" product.

It's hard to go through the financial pages without coming across a story about derivatives—those complex securities whose values are "derived" from other investments. One highly publicized victim of derivative investing was Orange County in California. The county had to file for bankruptcy primarily because of losses on derivatives in its investment portfolio.

The problems with derivatives bring up an important point: Investors should never invest in something they don't fully understand. That may sound simplistic, but you'd be surprised how many times investors buy an investment that they don't understand.

BOTTOM LINE: *It's better to invest in something in which you are familiar than to go for the "hottest" investment product.*

WHAT A DIFFERENCE A DAY MAKES

Big one-day declines in top-quality companies often provide excellent buying opportunities for long-term investors.

There's a school of thought that says that stocks are efficiently priced. In other words, a stock's price reflects the true value of the company, and searching for mispriced stocks is a waste of time. The fact that most professional money managers—supposedly experts in finding undervalued stocks—underperform the Standard & Poor's 500 index gives credence to the notion.

Yet, even if you buy the idea that a stock price is fairly representative of the true value of a company over time—and I would agree with that statement—the notion that a stock *always* reflects the fair value of the company is more difficult for me to swallow.

Take Philip Morris. On August 9, 1996, Wall Street shaved more than $11 billion off the value of the company.

$11 billion in one day.

Fueling the selling was a jury award in Florida favoring the plaintiff in a tobacco liability case. Obviously, the jury award held negative implications for the stock price. But $11 billion worth? Interestingly, following the decline, Philip Morris stock quickly gathered itself and, in the course of a few months, was selling at all-time highs.

If you don't buy the notion that stocks are always priced efficiently, then your major task as an investor is to exploit the opportunities when stocks may be mispriced—when investor emotions run to extremes and create, perhaps only for a moment, a solid buying opportunity.

I particularly like to buy when stocks decline sharply on news of lawsuits, labor strikes, and product tamperings. Such developments rarely leave a lasting imprint on the stock price.

THE DANGERS OF SELLING STOCK

Selling stock generates commissions and creates potential tax liabilities.

L ike many investors, you face a dilemma today: Should you sell and lock up your profits? Buy? Hold?

My experience, supported by reams of academic studies, tells me that you are much better off not trying to time purchases and sells on the basis of what you think the stock market is going to do. While you might get lucky occasionally, inevitably you are going to be wrong much more often than you're right.

I see literally hundreds of stock portfolios over the course of a year. The investors who are most successful are not those who start with the biggest investment nest eggs. They are those who implement a long-term accumulation program in good-quality stocks, keeping selling to a minimum.

Why is selling bad? Selling stock costs you money in commissions, which can erode the value of your investment. Furthermore, when selling a stock in which you have a profit, you are incurring a tax liability for that year instead of deferring your tax liability. Also keep in mind that most people sell stock for the wrong reasons. Many individual investors generally sell after the bad news is out and the stock is already discounting the bad news, which means selling at or near the bottom.

BOTTOM LINE: *If you buy right, you won't have to worry about selling.*

TAX SELLING

Don't let tax selling drive your investment decisions.

Toward the end of the year, investors' fancies usually turn to tax selling. If you are one of those investors who lets tax decisions dictate selling, beware—you may be making a big mistake.

All too often, I see investors base sell decisions strictly on the ability to capture a capital loss to offset capital gains. What investors should really be doing is assessing the ongoing potential of the stock, not what it has done in the past. It could very well be that the stock in which you have a loss is the stock best situated for gains over the next 12 months. You'd be better off buying more of the stock rather than selling to lock up a capital loss for tax purposes.

Future prospects of the stock should drive your sell decisions, not whether you have a gain or a loss.

GOOD REASONS FOR SELLING STOCK

The "stupid acquisition" is a good reason to sell.

There are legitimate reasons to sell stock, but they are few in number.

You shouldn't sell stock because you think the overall market is high. Selling individual stocks on the basis of timing market movements is a loser's game. You should never sell a stock merely because the stock has done well and seems "high." Nor should you sell a stock purely for tax purposes.

REMEMBER: *Selling stocks generates two unwanted consequences—transaction costs and potential tax liabilities. I'm not saying that you should never sell stocks. I am saying that you should sell sparingly.*

A good reason to sell is a deterioration in the company's financial position. You can check this by monitoring the firm's long-term debt levels. If debt levels are rising, trouble could be on the horizon. An additional reason to sell is what I call the "stupid acquisition." It's not a stretch to say that most companies overpay for acquisitions. Why? Unfortunately, CEOs' egos and empire building often supplant shareholders' interests. The result is that the acquirer pays more than the acquiree is worth. This is especially true when two or more companies compete for the same target.

Another reason to sell is that the original reason you bought the stock didn't pan out as you thought. Perhaps you bought a stock because you liked a new product. You soon realized that the new product was not competing as well as you thought. If your reasons for buying the stock never materialize, you're better off owning something else.

What about selling companies when their products become obsolete? Obviously, a company whose competitors have passed it by, technologically speaking, is a worthwhile sell candidate. The problem is that most investors aren't smart enough to keep up with the rapidly changing technologies in such fields as computers, electronics, and software. Therefore, they probably shouldn't be investing in these companies in the first place.

PREDICTING THE FUTURE WITH A REARVIEW MIRROR

Don't try to project the market's return for a given year on the basis of performance in the prior year.

You wouldn't drive your car looking exclusively out of the rearview mirror. Yet, many investors conduct their investment activities that way.

I can remember at the beginning of 1996 that many analysts felt the year would be a poor one because 1995 was so strong. The thinking was that you couldn't have two good years in a row. Of course, just because the stock market rose in 1995 didn't mean it couldn't rise in 1996. Many of the same factors that aided stocks in 1995—strong corporate earnings, low inflation, and favorable interest rates—looked as if they could persist in 1996. Yet I'm sure many investors ignored the positive fundamental factors, instead opting to use a rearview mirror to guide their portfolios in 1996.

What happened in 1996? The stock market rose 26 percent—not as much as the 33 percent advance in the Standard & Poor's 500 in 1995, but well above the market's long-term average annual return of less than 11 percent.

Don't try to project the market's return for a given year on the basis of performance in the prior year. Focus on the three factors that have the greatest effect on the market—earnings, interest rates, and inflation—and see if those characteristics are favorable or unfavorable.

DEFENSIVE STOCKS

Certain stocks have a tendency to hold up relatively well during market declines.

Typically, during periods of market uncertainty, investors flock to so-called defensive stocks. These stocks generally share such traits as consistent earnings growth, steady dividends, reasonable yields, and an ability to weather economic cycles. Traditional "defensive" industry groups include drugs and health care, consumer products, and electric and natural gas utilities.

Investors should understand that the defensive nature of some groups can change over time. Witness the big drop in electric utilities in recent years, as well as periodic volatility in the health-care sector due, in part, to uncertainties surrounding health-care reform. While it's safe to say that there probably is no such thing as a totally defensive group, certain industry groups should hold up reasonably well in the near future.

One industry likely to show above-average relative strength during market declines is the oil sector. In this sector, my favorite is Exxon.

MOMENTUM INVESTING

Momentum investors buy stocks showing superior price strength relative to the overall market.

What if I told you that one popular investment strategy centers around chasing stocks that are rising the fastest in price. The higher the stock rises, the more attractive it becomes. Such a strategy runs counter to that old Wall Street cliché: "Buy low, sell high." Yet momentum investing, as it is called, has produced some staggering returns in recent years.

The underlying basis of momentum investing is the following maxim: "The trend is your friend." Momentum investors buy stocks that show superior price strength relative to other stocks in the market, believing that the rising price trends will continue.

Notice that I've said nothing about earnings growth, financial positions, management expertise, or other fundamental factors. Momentum investors don't analyze a company's fundamental position. They ride the coattails of the stock's rising price.

The problem I see with momentum investing is that

you buy stocks that seem overpriced. Expensive stocks can become even more expensive during a bull market—and this is what momentum investors hope—but at some point the party stops. Think of momentum investing as a game of musical chairs. As you get further along in the game, the risks that you'll be the odd one out increase. Although momentum investing works well during up markets, it can be especially punishing during market corrections or bear markets. Why? Because the stocks that usually have the fastest run-ups during bull markets are the most vulnerable during market pullbacks.

If you employ momentum investing, understand that a key success factor is getting out before you're left holding the bag. Since exiting the stock requires you to time the market and your investments successfully—and few investors can do this consistently over time—momentum investing is a high-risk approach to investing in the market.

INVESTING IN "CRASH" STOCKS

When buying "crash" stocks, it's always best to be patient.

Everybody loves to invest in "crash" stocks—stocks that have fallen sharply from their previous highs. For investors trying to find the next Chrysler, here are some simple rules to follow:

- *Be patient.* It's better to wait for an ax to hit the ground than to try to catch it on the way down. The same logic applies to crash stocks. Make sure the stock has truly bottomed before buying. How do you know? One positive sign is to see the stock trade within a narrow price range—say 5 percent from the top of the range to the bottom—for several months. Such sideways trading is often a clue that a stock is bottoming. Don't buy a crash stock that is still trending lower.

- *Bet with the insiders.* Corporate insiders—such as executives, directors, and majority stockholders—presumably know more about a company than outside investors. If you see corporate insiders buying a stock that is dramatically depressed, chances are they are expecting a turnaround in the company's business. How do you know what insiders are doing? *The Wall Street Journal* reports on insider trading every Wednesday, and *Barron's* reports on it in every weekly issue.

- *Look for improving earnings momentum.* It is difficult for companies to sustain a rally without earnings momentum. That goes doubly for crash stocks. Earnings momentum doesn't mean that you have to wait until the company is showing positive quarterly earnings gains. Earnings momentum can mean that a company's losses are declining. You'll need earnings improvement in order for most crash stocks to pay off handsomely.

- *Bet on only strong balance sheets.* Avoid crash stocks whose debt is at huge levels. These companies will have a difficult time coming back.

HIGH DEBT, HIGH RISK

The speed at which businesses built on debt unravel is amazing.

One of my major investment tenets is to avoid companies with large debt burdens. There have been instances when this policy caused me to miss a few big winners. However, it has steered me clear of more than a few debacles through the years.

Why is debt such a problem for corporations? The biggest reason is the unrelenting nature of interest payments. When things are going well, servicing the debt isn't a problem. However, if business goes down the tubes for any extended period of time, a firm can get in trouble quickly.

The speed at which businesses built on debt unravel has always amazed me. That's why it's important to focus attention on those companies with moderate long-term debt levels. To determine a company's debt level, divide its long-term debt by total capitalization (total capitalization is long-term debt plus shareholder equity). I become concerned when I see this level go north of 50 percent. Look at this percentage over time and be especially cautious about buying a stock where debt levels are rising.

OPTION INVESTING (IS) FOR DUMMIES

Leave option investing to the so-called professionals.

Want to know how to make $1 million in the options market?

Start with $2 million.

Feel free to ignore my Jackie Mason impersonation, but don't ignore the advice—investing in the options markets is a loser's game.

We discussed earlier how options are used to hedge a portfolio, which is a risk reduction strategy. Many investors, however, speculate in options, and this investment practice is extremely risky.

As previously discussed, two popular options are call options and put options. A call option gives the holder the option of buying a particular stock at a given price. The option has a certain expiration period. For example, investors can buy a call option on IBM that gives you the option of buying IBM stock at a given price for a period of time. Rarely, however, do investors exercise the option to buy the common shares. Rather, investors buy options for the price appreciation of the option.

Here's a simple example of how a call option works. Let's say that IBM is trading for $150 per share. You buy a call option that allows you to buy IBM stock at $155 any time within, say, a three-month period (call options usually have three-, six-, or nine-month expiration periods). Now, to buy the call option will cost you something. In this example, with the stock currently selling below the option "exercise" price of $155, the option has no intrinsic value. However, because you have time on your side, the option has time value. Thus, let's say you pay $1 for an option (an option selling for $1 will cost you $100). Suddenly, IBM develops the hottest computer around, and the stock soars to $200 before your option expires. What can you expect the price of your option to do? Remember that the option gives you the ability to buy the stock at $155. With the stock trading at $200, the value of your option must be at least $45 ($200 - $155). You just saw the value of your option soar from $100 to $4,500!

A put option works the same way, except in reverse. You buy a put option on a stock that you think is heading south. The value of your put increases the more the stock slides.

Judging from the ability to leverage small investments into a killing, calls and puts sound too good to be true, right?

Unfortunately, rare is the options trader who pulls off such a coup. In fact, most options expire worthless. The problem with options is that not only do you have to be right about the direction of the stock; you also need to be perfect concerning the timing of the move.

Another factor to consider in purchasing options is the brokerage commission, which can be rather steep if you are buying just a few options. I once bought a couple of call options on an airline stock. I came to work one morning to see that the stock had jumped on takeover news, lifting my options with it. When I sold my options, I was distressed to learn that, after paying commissions on the buy and sell side plus taxes on the gain, I walked away with only a few bucks. I made a pact with myself never to buy another option as a speculation.

I suggest you do the same.

BEWARE OF "CAN'T MISS" INVESTMENTS

Investments that guarantee to return at least your principal after a certain time carry with them opportunity costs.

There aren't many free lunches in the financial markets, so beware when something sounds like a can't-miss investment.

For example, there are investments being sold that guarantee investors the return of at least their initial investment after 10 years. You can't lose, right? You can lose plenty in the form of lost interest earned and other opportunity costs. At just a 7 percent annual return, an investment doubles in 10 years.

The guaranteed-investment approach does provide an interesting investment opportunity for more speculative investors. Let's say you have $100,000 to invest and you want to be on the aggressive side. You can guarantee yourself at least $100,000 at the end of, say, 10 years by taking half the money and investing in a 10-year zero-coupon bond yielding 7 percent.

In 10 years, that $50,000 will grow to $100,000. With the other $50,000, you may want to try your luck at buying aggressive growth stocks. Even if you lose the entire $50,000, you'll still have the $100,000 in bonds at the end of 10 years.

CORPORATE SPIN-OFFS

Don't be so quick to sell shares obtained in a spin-off.

I've gotten many calls from investors who don't know what to do with the shares in new companies they have been receiving because of the plethora of corporate spin-offs.

The tendency among investors is to sell the new shares, since (1) they don't know much about the companies and (2) what good is holding 25 or 35 shares of a stock? Spin-offs usually result in holding odd lots (fewer than 100 shares) of the new company.

MY ADVICE: Don't be so quick to sell the new shares. Spin-offs represent interesting investments for several reasons.

First, a company that is now out from under a large corporation has the chance to flex its entrepreneurial muscles—something it might not have been able to do as part of a bigger entity.

Second, managers running the show now understand it is sink-or-swim time since the larger parent will no longer be subsidizing the firm. Having your back against the wall is often the best motivator.

Third, spin-offs are often depressed initially after being spun off, since many investors dump the shares, providing downward pressure on prices. However, once the selling has run its course, these shares have the ability to bounce nicely.

Finally, because they lack history, spin-offs are often difficult for Wall Street to evaluate. Thus, the opportunity exists for the spin-off to surprise analysts with better-than-expected earnings.

One spin-off that seems especially attractive is Lucent Technologies. Formerly under the AT&T umbrella, this producer of telecommunications equipment now has the ability to market its products to any and all telecommunications companies. Another spin-off that bears watching is NCR, also a former unit of AT&T. This producer of ATMs and data warehousing systems has favorable one-to three-year prospects.

STOCKS AND INFLATION

It's tough to beat stocks for keeping ahead of inflation.

A study by Pioneer Group, a financial-services firm, reflects the inflation-beating ability of Dow stocks. The study showed that from the end of 1974 to the end of 1994, only one of the 30 Dow components—Bethlehem Steel—failed to beat the cost of living.

The Dow's top five performers during that time were Boeing (average annual rate of return of 25 percent for the period), Coca-Cola (21 percent), Disney (21 percent), Philip Morris (20 percent), and Exxon (nearly 18 percent). At the bottom of the heap were Bethlehem Steel (1.6 percent: Bethlehem was removed from the Dow Industrials Average in 1997), IBM (7 percent), Eastman Kodak (8.4 percent), Caterpillar (9 percent), and Sears, Roebuck (10 percent).

The cost of living increased roughly 5 percent a year over the 20-year time frame.

PLAYING OVERSEAS MARKETS

One way to play overseas markets is by investing in U.S. firms with strong overseas distribution channels.

The potential benefits from overseas investing are substantial. Nevertheless, there are some things investors should know before dropping their dollars in overseas firms. First, you become a slave to exchange rates when you invest in another country. Second, accounting differences between domestic and overseas companies make stock analyses tricky.

Ways exist to play the overseas market without investing in foreign countries. One attractive way is to focus on U.S. firms that should capitalize on overseas opportunities. Consideration should be given to companies that are marketing-driven and have established overseas channels, such as top consumer-products firms Colgate-Palmolive and Procter & Gamble.

Another interesting way to play overseas markets is by investing in companies with a time-tested domestic idea that can be applied overseas. In this category is McDonald's, which should benefit nicely from overseas expansion.

MONOPOLY STOCKS

Companies with virtual monopolies are often immune to pricing pressures.

One strategy I like is to invest in companies that have a virtual monopoly in their business or, at the very least, a strong market position. Companies with virtual monopolies are immune to a certain extent to competition and have strong pricing power. Such companies generally ride through recessions relatively unscathed.

One example of a company with a strong market position is Service Corp. International. The firm is the largest operator of funeral services and cemeteries in the country and has been growing through acquisitions. Because of demographics, demand for funeral services should grow over the next several decades, which means the stock price should trend upward.

THE DOLLAR AND STOCK VALUES

A persistently weak dollar is often viewed as inflationary, since it boosts the prices of imports.

A weak dollar often is perceived as bad news for the stock market. A weak dollar raises the prices of imports, causing upward pressure on the inflation rate. A weak dollar also suggests that global investors believe the U.S. monetary system is too loose. One response to a weak dollar and heightened inflation expectations is for the Federal Reserve Board to lift interest rates—a move that helps support the dollar (higher interest rates draw foreign investors to the dollar) but hurts stocks.

Of course, not everybody is a loser from a weaker dollar. Firms with large overseas operations benefit from a weaker dollar, since their products are more competitively priced abroad.

What's an investor to do when the dollar is falling? A portfolio favoring multinational corporations should do well in such an environment.

HOW TO BUY A $5 STOCK

Diversification is an excellent way to lower risk when investing in $5 stocks.

The appeal of $5 stocks is fairly obvious, particularly for individual investors with limited funds. However, investing in such low-priced stocks can be fraught with risks for uneducated investors. Fortunately, ways exist to reduce the risks and enhance the potential for success.

- *Diversify.* It is important to diversify among $5 stocks, since you'll likely get a clunker or two in the group.

- *Buy for value, not price.* Even at $5, a stock can be overpriced. Investors should use earnings momentum, financial strength, and other traditional yardsticks to pick a $5 stock.

- *Limit exposure.* For a relatively aggressive investor, $5 stocks should be limited to a maximum of roughly 5 percent to 10 percent of the total portfolio.

- *Protect profits.* Consider taking partial profits more quickly, since $5 stocks tend to be volatile.

- *Look for strong finances.* A small company with a strong financial position has the ability to weather rough times in its markets.

TIME DIVERSIFICATION THROUGH DOLLAR-COST AVERAGING

Dollar-cost averaging means that you make fixed dollar investments on a regular basis in a particular stock or fund.

To properly diversify across assets means, in a nutshell, to spread your money across a variety of investments. In that way, poor performance in one investment can be offset by gains in another investment.

While diversification usually refers to "what" you buy—stocks, bonds, mutual funds—diversification can also apply to "how" you buy. For example, investing all your money at once leaves you vulnerable to committing your assets at what might turn out to be the exact worst time to be investing. Conversely, perhaps you'll get lucky and pick the absolute best time to be buying stocks. Nevertheless, it seems a riskier proposition to pick a single point in time to invest. I'd rather employ time diversification by spreading out my investments over time.

An excellent tool for time diversification is "dollar-cost averaging." Dollar-cost averaging means that you make fixed dollar investments on a regular basis, perhaps every month or every quarter. The beauty of dollar-cost averaging is that it forces you to buy more shares when stocks are cheaper and fewer shares when stocks are more expensive. Another benefit is that dollar-cost averaging strips all emotion and market timing from a portfolio.

Here's how dollar-cost averaging works. Let's say you buy $500 worth of McDonald's stock every month in a dollar-cost averaging program. The first month, the stock trades for $50 per share. You invest $500 to buy 10 shares of McDonald's. The next month, McDonald's trades for $40 per share. Your $500 monthly investment now buys 12.5 shares of McDonald's. (You can buy fractional shares of stock if you employ dollar-cost averaging in a company's dividend reinvestment plan.) In month 3, McDonald's jumps to $48 per share. Your $500 investment buys 10.4 shares. In month 4, McDonald's returns to the $50 level, whereby your $500 investment buys 10 shares of stock. At the end of four months, you've invested $2,000 to buy 42.9 shares, giving yourself an average cost of $46.63 per share. Yet McDonald's is trading at the same $50 price it was four months ago. The fact that you bought more shares when the stock dipped is the reason you are sitting with a profit on your investment even though McDonald's has registered no net gain in stock price in the four-month period.

Of course, dollar-cost averaging in a stock that goes from $40 to $4 and never rebounds can be devastating to a portfolio. Focus any dollar-cost averaging strategy on stocks that have outstanding finances, solid track records of dividend and earnings growth, and industry-leading positions. Avoid dollar-cost averaging with penny stocks and other high-risk stocks.

VALUE AVERAGING

With value averaging, you know how much your portfolio will be worth at the end of the investment period, but you don't know how much it will cost out of your pocket.

A sister investment strategy to dollar-cost averaging is "value averaging."

Value averaging says that, instead of making the same investment each month in a stock or mutual fund, you vary the amount invested so that the value of the portfolio increases by a fixed sum or percentage each interval.

Let's say that, instead of investing $500 each month, you want the value of your investment to rise by $500 each month. In the first month, the value of your portfolio rises $200. Under value averaging, you add $300 to the investment to achieve your plan of having the investment increase $500 each month. Now, let's say that the investment increases $600 in a given month. Since you want the investment to rise only $500, you sell $100 worth of the investment. Conversely, let's say the value of the investment drops $200 in a given month. Since you want the value of the investment to rise $500 each month, you contribute $700 for that month—$200 to offset the loss plus $500 to increase the value of the portfolio.

An easy way to compare value averaging with dollar-cost averaging is to think in the following terms:

- With dollar-cost averaging, you know how much you'll invest, but you don't know what the value will be at the end of your investment horizon.

- With value averaging, you know how much your portfolio will be worth at the end of your investment horizon, but you don't know how much it will cost out of your pocket.

Michael Edleson, who popularized value averaging with his book *Value Averaging: The Safe and Easy Strategy for Higher Investment Returns* (International Publishing) ran 50 computer simulations over a variety of five-year market periods. More than 90 percent of the time, value averaging outperformed dollar-cost averaging.

Still, between dollar-cost averaging and value averaging, I lean toward the former. I regard value averaging as a more aggressive strategy than dollar-cost averaging, since the total amount of your investment is not constrained, as it is under dollar-cost averaging. Value averaging will create more transaction costs, since you may have to sell shares to stay within your parameters. And since you're selling stock, you're incurring potential tax liabilities. Value averaging also requires more monitoring than a basic dollar-cost averaging program.

I BOUGHT THE COMPANY

Investors would make dramatically different investment decisions if they bought stocks on the basis of whether they actually wanted to own the company, not the stock.

Some of you probably remember those commercials several years ago featuring Victor Kiam, the former owner of Remington, who boasted about the company's shaver, "I liked the product so much, I bought the company."

Individual investors would do well to follow Kiam's example.

Buying stocks in companies that produce products you like is an excellent way to pick stocks. Why? If you like a product, chances are you're not alone. And if you use a product and see a deterioration in product quality over time, you're probably way ahead of so-called Wall Street experts who are good with numbers—numbers, by the way, that can be manipulated by companies in the short run—but who may have no clue as to what consumers are thinking about the product.

Taking Kiam's comments further, I maintain that investors would make dramatically different investment decisions if they bought a stock on the basis of whether they actually wanted to own the company, not the stock. Few investors regard stock ownership as true ownership in a company. If more investors approached stock picking as a choice of which companies they'd like to own outright, better decisions would be made.

For example, would you want to be in charge of Coca-Cola? Or would you rather own a steel company? If someone said you could own any retailer, would you choose Kmart? Or Nordstrom?

Of course, I know you cannot ignore price. If a steel company were available for 50 cents on the dollar, who wouldn't want to own it, right? Unfortunately, most of us don't know enough about the steel industry to tell whether a company is cheap or not. I do, however, feel I have a pretty good handle on whether Walgreen, the drugstore chain and one of my favorite stocks, is doing well (just drive by its parking lots and see all the cars). That's why I stick with companies in which I can get my arms around their business.

As one of my colleagues puts it so aptly, "Buy companies, not stocks." You'll be better off in the long run.

STOCKS WITH "KICKERS"

A kicker could be unappreciated assets, a management change, or business restructuring.

One of my favorite stock-picking strategies is to pick stocks with "kickers." Kickers represent assets or potential events that could boost the stock price. What are some common kickers?

- *Salable assets.* Wall Street likes to see companies sell assets, and firms with sprawling operations have the ability to generate investor interest by announcing asset sales.

- *Management changes*. Wall Street looks favorably on underperforming companies that experience management changes.

- *Unappreciated assets*. An unappreciated asset may be appreciated real estate kept on the company's books at cost, an equity stake in a fast-growing company, or a small business segment experiencing rapid growth.

Patience is usually required when investing in stocks with kickers. Especially if you're investing on the basis of unappreciated assets, it may take some time for others on Wall Street to appreciate the company.

AVOID UNCLE SAM

Deferring taxes has a powerful impact on a portfolio over time.

Some of the biggest fortunes on Wall Street are made one crumb at a time.

Investors who can earn just 1 percent a month will double their investment every six years. One way investors can eke out extra gains is by deferring taxes on investments as long as possible. One reason I prefer stocks over mutual funds is that, with stocks, I control my tax destiny. I incur a tax liability only if I decide to sell my shares. That's not the case with mutual funds.

Mutual-fund investors are at the mercy of the fund manager, who can force a tax liability on fundholders by distributing capital gains. It is especially aggravating when you are sitting with a paper loss in a mutual fund yet have to pay taxes on a capital-gain distribution that you received during the year.

The ability to defer taxes indefinitely via stock ownership can have a powerful impact on a portfolio over time. Without having to share gains with Uncle Sam by not selling, you can watch your entire investment continue to compound year in and year out.

Deferring taxes should allow you to earn at least an extra percent or so a year on your portfolio. While that may not seem like much, remember: Those crumbs add up over time.

BUYING NEW ISSUES

Most high-quality new issues are never available to individual investors.

Many of you probably read in the financial papers the story of Netscape, the Internet company. On the first day of trading, the stock jumped from $28 to as high as $75 before closing the day at just over $58—more than a 100 percent gain in one day.

I'm sure that to many people, Netscape shows just how easy it is to make money in the new-issues market. Just buy the stock at the initial public offering price and hold it for a day or so. Let me tell you—it's just not that easy.

First, for most investors, getting shares in "hot" new issues is virtually impossible. Indeed, shares for the very best new issues are reserved for big institutional investors. Small investors never get a shot at the good ones. Second, studies have shown that new issues fall as fast as they rise.

The following rules should be followed by investors considering new issues:

- If your broker calls you offering a "hot" new issue, run for your life. New issues that are marketed to the masses are merchandise that has already been passed over by the big guys and is probably junk. Take a pass.

- Never buy a new issue from a cold-calling broker. Penny-stock dealers work this way, and investors who buy these offerings rarely do well over time.

- Read the prospectus carefully. The prospectus will tell you some important items: how much time the main players will be devoting to the business, executive compensation levels, and so on.

- It's never a good idea to chase new issues. In the case of Netscape, investors who bought shares at the day's high of roughly $75 were sitting with a 17-point loss at day's end. Better to wait until the stock trades lower— often new issues will return to their initially offered price if you wait long enough—before buying.

WHEN BAD NEWS IS GOOD NEWS (FOR STOCK-HOLDERS)

Wall Street generally rewards companies which demonstrate they can do more with fewer workers.

To some individuals, it seems the market rewards bad news and penalizes good news. This is clearly the case concerning the job outlook. Strong job creation causes investors to sell stocks, while corporate layoffs bring out the buyers.

There is a reason for this seemingly perverse relationship. Three factors have fueled the stock market to all-time highs—low interest rates, low inflation, and steadily growing (but not hypergrowing) corporate profits. Notice that "strong job creation" is not in the mix. In fact, sizable job creation can work against these factors in the following ways.

The creation of a lot of new jobs means that the economy is growing rapidly and companies are expanding. In order to expand, companies need to borrow money. Rising demand for money often raises the cost of money (i.e., interest rates). A strong economy can often lead to higher interest rates, which is a negative for stocks.

A strong economy, as well as big job growth, can put upward pressure on the general price level and wages. Upward pressure on prices and wages is inflationary, which is another negative. Conversely, companies announcing layoffs are demonstrating to Wall Street that they are tightening their belts and becoming more efficient. Wall Street loves efficiency and generally rewards companies that show they can do more with less.

"LADDERING" BOND INVESTMENTS

Laddering means to stagger the maturities of your bond holdings.

B ond investing during an environment of interest-rate uncertainties presents a number of problems. Since bond prices drop when interest rates rise, buying bonds during a period of rising rates is generally not a good idea.

Because of the interest-sensitive nature of bonds, some investors choose a "laddering" technique when buying individual bonds. Laddering your bonds means to stagger the maturity dates, say, for each year for five years. If interest rates are rising, you are annually selling off bonds and reinvesting the proceeds at higher yields. Laddering can also be an effective strategy if rates are falling, but its major use is to protect a bond portfolio when rates are rising.

Investors who don't want to buy individual bonds can use the laddering approach with bond mutual funds with different average maturities. However, using funds provides much less precision to a laddering program.

BUYING STOCKS AT A DISCOUNT

Through certain dividend reinvestment plans, it is possible to buy stock cheaper than the market price.

A way exists to buy certain stocks at a discount to their market price—but don't expect to hear about it from your broker.

As explained in Chapter 4, dividend reinvestment plans (DRIPs) allow investors to buy stock directly from the company, without a broker. One attractive feature of over 100 reinvestment plans is the ability to purchase stock at discounts to the market price. These discounts range from 3 percent to 5 percent of the market price.

A number of real estate investment trusts (REITs), banks, and utilities offer DRIP discounts. Such discounts can boost the yield of a stock. For example, UtiliCorp United, an electric utility, offers a 5 percent discount in its DRIP. Because DRIP participants have dividends reinvested at the discount, the effective yield for these investors is higher than the yield for investors who buy UtiliCorp outside the DRIP.

Investors who are interested in DRIP discounts should contact companies of interest for prospectuses, which will explain the plans and indicate if discounts are available. Also, my book *Buying Stocks Without a Broker* (McGraw-Hill) has a complete listing of DRIP discounts along with telephone numbers.

CONFUSION MEANS OPPORTUNITY

Often, the best opportunities on Wall Street are the most confusing.

The stock market is fairly "efficient." Since so many smart people are searching for good values, most stocks are priced fairly close to their "true" value.

Since stocks are often efficiently priced, some of the best opportunities in the market are in stocks which are difficult to analyze, perhaps because of a corporate restructuring or acquisition. Uncertainty makes it difficult to value a company properly, which leaves room for market "inefficiencies."

One stock with a lot of uncertainty is Westinghouse Electric. The company's CBS acquisition created a real wild card for analysts to evaluate going forward. Since there is a lot of uncertainty surrounding Westinghouse, there is also the opportunity for the company to surprise analysts with stronger-than-expected earnings. I've been buying Westinghouse and recommend these shares for more aggressive investors.

"MUST HAVE" INDUSTRY GROUPS

All investors should have representation in a few key industry groups, such as telecommunications equipment and information services.

Investors who look for companies with accelerating earnings growth usually find stock-market winners. Of course, finding companies with superior earnings power is easier said than done. However, if you think in terms of what industries are destined to grow over the next 10 years, the task becomes easier.

Here are a few of the industry groups that every investor should have in a portfolio:

- *Telecommunications equipment.* While it is unclear which companies will be the winners and losers among telecommunications providers, it is clear that the world's telecommunications infrastructure will have to be upgraded. Huge growth in data and telephone transmissions and the need for improved telecommunication services in developing countries point to big demand for companies that provide the backbone for our global telecommunications network. In this group, I own Lucent Technologies, the AT&T spin-off. Now that the firm is out from under Ma Bell's wing, Lucent can market its wares to any and all telecommunications companies. With the research firepower of Bell Laboratories behind it, this company should be a player in every facet of the telecommunications revolution.

- *Information services.* Information is power, and our thirst for knowledge is far from being sated. Companies providing information to companies and consumers should continue to do well. Two information services firms that I own are Equifax, a leading provider of credit-information services, and Reuters Holdings, the United Kingdom-based provider of financial-information services.

- *Business services.* If you believe in the entrepreneurial spirit in America, it follows that new-business creation will continue at a rapid clip. Companies that are particularly adept at performing necessary but painful tasks for businesses will be in demand as the shape and size of the future corporation takes on a decidedly smaller look. One firm I own is Paychex. This Nasdaq-traded stock is the leading provider of payroll-processing services for small and medium-size businesses. Earnings have been growing at a rapid rate, and long-term growth potential is excellent.

- *Security services.* Consumers and businesses are demanding improved security services to protect their businesses, homes, possessions, and even their data and corporate intelligence. Firms in these markets should experience healthy demand. I particularly like Pittston Brink's, which provides consumer as well as business security services.

- *Agriculture.* As emerging countries grow and prosper, demand for agricultural products will accelerate. In this group, I particularly like fertilizer companies, such as Norsk Hydro, a Norwegian enterprise.

MERGER MANIA

Regulatory changes are just one of the factors fueling merger activity.

From technology to banking, merger activity has occurred in a host of industries over the last few years. Why?

First, the sharp rise in the stock market has lifted the value of many shares—shares which are now being used to buy other companies. Many deals are being done with stock that is now more valuable as a result of the bull market.

Second, interest rates, relatively speaking, are still low. Thus, the cost of bank borrowings is sufficient to support deals.

Third, regulatory changes, most notably in the banking and utility sectors, are driving mergers.

Where will future mergers likely occur? Among regulated industries, look for activity to remain strong in banking and heat up in utilities and telephone stocks. Also, look for further bargains in the technology sector, especially as more companies use their inflated stocks to do deals.

PICKING ELECTRIC UTILITY STOCKS

Utilities with low-cost positions and growing nonutility operations are best situated for long-term gains.

Electric utilities have taken it on the chin over the last year. The drop is no doubt surprising to many investors who purchased utilities thinking they were surrogates for certificates of deposit and other fixed-income investments. However, given a rapidly changing regulatory environment, utilities are no longer "widow and orphan" stocks.

The best utility investments share the following characteristics:

- *Low-cost electricity.* Utilities that have low electricity costs, especially low industrial electricity prices, will be able to weather increased competition in their markets.

- *Strong nonutility operations.* Many utilities got into outside businesses only to find the results disappointing. However, a few, such as TECO Energy, have done well in businesses outside the utility field. Such success will be even more important as rates of return in the utility sector are crimped.

- *Geographic diversification.* Having operations in a variety of geographic regions can help shield a firm from damaging regulatory rulings in any one area. Citizens

Utilities is a good example of geographic diversification. The firm provides electric, gas, and telephone services in 22 states.

- *Low payout ratios.* The payout ratio is the company's dividend divided by its 12-month earnings per share. A high payout ratio—a payout ratio of 1.0 means a company is paying out all its earnings in dividends—indicates less room to expand the dividend in the future. Concentrate on utilities with payout ratios below 0.8.

REIT INVESTING

REITs have been gaining favor with income investors, but you don't want a large exposure to this group.

Real estate investment trusts (REITs) have been gaining investor attention of late. However, before you buy an REIT, you should at least know what you're buying.

REITs are publicly traded trusts which pool investors' funds to invest in various types of properties, from mixes of commercial retail and office space to investments exclusively in medical facilities. The cash flows from the real estate are passed to the shareholders of the REIT.

Over the years, REITs have suffered when commercial real estate slumped. A rebound in real estate, coupled with the relatively high yields many REITs are paying, has brought investors back to these shares.

REITs frequently trimmed dividends in the past when real estate markets turned down. Still, diversifying a portfolio with REITs has appeal, but investors should not load up on these investments.

Among REITs, two worth considering are Duke Realty Investments and United Mobile Homes. Duke Realty provides leasing and management services to a diversified portfolio of properties located primarily in the Midwest. United Mobile Homes owns and operates mobile home parks.

CYCLICAL STOCKS

For long-term investors, representation in cyclicals should be limited.

C yclical stocks are issues that are the most vulnerable to downturns in the economy. They include housing, construction, heavy equipment, and auto issues.

These stocks tend to do well when the economy comes out of a recession. My feeling about cyclicals is that, for long-term investors, their presence in a portfolio should be limited. While these issues represent excellent trading vehicles, too many cyclical stocks have shown large price swings on a year-to-year basis and very little sustained upward price action over time.

If you are a buy-and-hold investor, especially if you hold stocks for 5 to 10 years or longer, it makes more sense to focus on issues in which annual earnings growth is generally achieved and vulnerability to cyclical downturns is limited. These companies usually have stock prices which show much better long-term appreciation.

If you buy cyclical stocks, focus on what I call "growth" cyclicals. These are firms that have businesses tied to the economic cycle but that manage to show steady earnings growth over time. Growth cyclicals that are particularly attractive are Emerson Electric and Grainger (W. W.). Emerson Electric produces electronics and electrical equipment. Grainger is a leading distributor of electrical supplies and equipment.

STOCKS FOR THE GRAYING OF AMERICA

Leisure services and drugstore chains are two investment plays on the graying of America.

Playing demographic trends is one way to invest for the long term. One demographic trend that receives much attention is the graying of America. The most obvious plays on this market are drug and health-care companies, which will likely see increased demand for products and services from an aging population. But there are other ways to play this trend.

For example, the cruise industry is popular with senior citizens, and Carnival offers an interesting play in this area. Also, an older population, sad to say, implies greater demand for funeral services. Service Corp. International is a leading provider of funeral services and should see its business improve.

The drugmakers are direct beneficiaries of an aging population, and so are the companies that provide the prescription drugs. In this category, Walgreen, the drugstore chain, is a leader in prescription drug fulfillment and has attractive long-term prospects.

LIGHT-BLUE CHIPS

Light-blue chips represent the blue chips of tomorrow.

It's every investor's dream to find the next GE or Intel. One hunting ground is among stocks that I classify as "light-blue chips." These are companies that lack the size and seasoning of today's blue chips but have the potential to be tomorrow's leaders. Light-blue chips share a number of characteristics:

- Outstanding financial positions, highlighted by manageable debt levels, ample cash flow, and strong liquidity. Such a financial posture provides the needed resources to continue growing internally and via acquisitions.

- Leadership positions in attractive market niches. Strong market positions shield the firms from competition while allowing them to weather economic cycles.

- High and rising net profit margins, attractive returns on equity, and solid earnings growth.

One example of a light-blue chip that I've already discussed is Paychex, which trades on the Nasdaq market. The company is a leading provider of payroll-processing services for small and medium-size businesses. Paychex has a strong market niche and a stellar record of sales and earnings growth. The stock is rarely cheap. Nevertheless, I like the issue's long-term prospects. I own these shares and recommend them for growth investors.

DIVIDENDS EVERY MONTH

By owning the right basket of stocks, investors can receive a dividend check every month.

A dividend check is certainly a welcome event, particularly for investors who need dividends to supplement their incomes.

Corporations pay dividends only once every three months. However, it is possible to receive a dividend check every month with the proper basket of stocks. For example, consider some of the companies that comprise the Dow Jones Industrial Average. Eastman Kodak, General Electric, and Sears, Roebuck & Company pay dividends every January, April, July, and October. On the other hand, Dow stocks American Express, AT&T, and

Procter & Gamble pay dividends every February, May, August, and November. And Exxon, General Motors, and IBM pay dividends every March, June, September, and December.

By owning stocks from each of the three groups, an investor would receive a dividend check every month of the year.

While a dividend-payment schedule should not be the overriding factor in stock selection, it should at least be considered when you are building a portfolio primarily for income.

FOOL'S GOLD

All that glitters is not gold stocks.

During a time when most stocks have posted huge gains, gold shares have stunk up a portfolio over the last decade. One reason for the poor performance of gold is the low-inflation environment which has characterized the economy over the last several years. Gold is often viewed as an inflation hedge; no inflation means no reason to own gold stocks.

You would think that after years of lousy performance, gold would not be high on most investors' hit parade.

You'd be wrong.

Big numbers of gold "bugs" still seem to exist. These investment masochists continue to believe that one day gold will come back and they'll be able to say, "We told you so." Of course, gold investors have been saying for years that gold is ready to take off, but promise has not met reality.

As you can tell, I'm not a big fan of gold stocks. To have a small portion of a portfolio devoted to precious metals—perhaps 5 percent—makes some sense from a diversification standpoint. But to have much more than that is the wrong way to go, in my opinion.

If you must invest in a metals stock, try a diversified company such as Norsk Hydro. This Norwegian-based concern has metal assets in addition to oil and gas and fertilizer operations. The stock provides a good way to play the natural-resources markets without all the risks of investing in a pure metals play.

BANDWAGON INVESTING

Investors should avoid bandwagon stocks; buy only after they've corrected.

Some individual investors have a habit of jumping on the investment bandwagon right when it's about to get a flat. Their timing is usually late and comes after the stock already has jumped higher to reflect the good news.

A good example of bandwagon investing was Internet stocks. Some Internet firms are likely to show good growth over time. Nevertheless, stock prices for Internet stocks already reflected the possibility of increased business by the time the media focused on the group.

Does that mean an investor should avoid such band-wagon investment opportunities? Yes, at least initially when the stocks have run up sharply. A more sane approach is to try to buy these issues during price pull-backs. Stay with high-quality issues when pursuing hot investment areas. Such stocks should do well even if the hype surrounding the bandwagon investment opportunity remains just that—hype.

7
MUTUAL FUNDS

There are more than $3 trillion in mutual funds. While that figure is astounding enough, think of all the fees being generated by that money. If you estimate that the average mutual fund charges investors 1 percent of their assets per year (and that figure may be on the low side), the total amount of fees that mutual-fund families receive annually is a staggering $30 billion.

The question you should now be asking yourself is this:

"What do investors get for their money?"

Unfortunately, too often what that $30 billion in annual fees buys is mediocre performance. For example, according to Morningstar, the mutual-fund rating service, more than 80 percent of all diversified equity mutual funds underperformed the Standard & Poor's 500 in 1995.

You might be saying to yourself, "OK, but 1995

was an unusually good year for the market. What about a tough year for stocks? I bet mutual funds hold up better in down markets."

Let's look at 1994, a sluggish year for the market overall. According to Morningstar, more than 70 percent of diversified funds underperformed the S&P 500 in 1994. And the performance of mutual funds versus the S&P 500 wasn't much better in 1996.

To be fair, there have been years when equity mutual funds, as a group, outperformed the market. However, suffice it to say that, at least over the last few years, few mutual-fund investors have gotten their money's worth from the fees they pay.

As you can tell, I'm not a cheerleader for the mutual-fund industry. Yes, I do believe mutual funds can be worthwhile investments (I even own some funds), and funds and stocks can coexist profitably in a portfolio. However, I think investors need to approach fund investing with a healthy skepticism.

This chapter examines the pros and cons of fund investing. Topics include mutual-fund selection, the costs of mutual funds, taxes and mutual funds, and fund diversification.

FUND "CARRYING" CHARGES

Those annual "carrying" charges to own a mutual fund can add up over several years.

Over the last decade, most investors probably didn't pay a lot of attention to how much they paid in fees to mutual-fund companies, brokers, and other financial-services firms. When you earn 18 percent to 20 percent a year on your money, who cares about a 1 percent or 2 percent fee?

The problem is that, if we return to more historical returns of 10 percent or lower, those fees could mean the difference between a portfolio that prospers and one that goes under water.

One way to look at fees is as "opportunity" costs. A fee you pay this year hurts returns not only for year one but also for every subsequent year, since the money you pay in fees will never earn a dime. For example, it's typical that an investor with $10,000 in a mutual fund will pay $150 or more per year in fees. What's the real value of that $150? Over a 20-year period, $150 per year at 9 percent annual interest comes out to be more than $8,300 in money "lost" to fees.

Here's another example. Let's take two $50,000 portfolios. One is a buy-and-hold portfolio in stocks. The other is a general equity mutual fund. The stock portfolio and the mutual fund, over a 20-year period, both post an average annual return—before "carrying costs"—of 11 percent. How much would you have in each portfolio at the end of 20 years? In the stock portfolio—the portfolio with no carrying costs—you would have over $403,000. In the mutual-fund portfolio—a portfolio with annual fees of 1.5 percent of fund assets—you'd have approximately $300,000. That's a difference of more than $100,000.

Remember that the next time you think mutual-fund fees don't matter.

BEWARE OF FUND MARKETING

In an era in which there are more mutual funds than listed stocks, it becomes important to do your homework before investing.

The heavy marketing battle in the mutual-fund industry has important implications for individual investors. It has been argued that it's not necessarily the best mutual funds that garner investors' money; it's the mutual funds with the deepest pockets for advertising and marketing. It's likely that the big will get bigger; smaller mutual funds will either fall by the wayside or be gobbled up by bigger competitors—the latter a trend that's already occurring.

Bottom line for investors: It's not necessarily the mutual fund that stuffs your mailbox with the most promotional material that's the best investment. In an era in which there are more mutual funds than listed stocks, it becomes critically important to do your homework before buying a mutual fund.

Items to consider before investing include:

- What are the load fees as well as annual management fees?

- How long has the current fund manager been running the fund?

- What is the breadth of research done by the firm—is it a "one star" shop or is there a team of analysts?

- What is the size of the fund? Large funds may have more difficulty getting in and out of certain stocks.

WORDS TO LIVE BY

When in doubt, stick with no-load funds.

With many investors picking mutual funds as their investment of choice, here are a few of my "words to live by" when it comes to mutual funds:

- Don't chase the winning mutual funds. This year's winner could be next year's loser, especially if it is a sector fund that did well merely because its industry group was hot. Pick funds that match your investment objectives and are compatible with your investment ideas.

- When in doubt, stick with no-load funds. There is no conclusive evidence indicating that load funds out-perform no-load funds.

- Don't be lulled into a false sense of security just because you've invested in a mutual fund. Bear markets bite mutual funds just as hard as they do stocks.

FINDING A GOOD STOCK MUTUAL FUND

Consider the size of the fund's asset base when selecting a fund investment.

It's never been easy to find a winning mutual fund, and the ever-increasing number of funds makes the task that much harder. Nevertheless, here's a way to increase your odds.

Few mutual-fund experts and managers would dispute the notion that size matters in the mutual-fund arena. It does, but not in a good way. A fund with assets of $5 million is a whole lot easier to manage than a fund with $5 billion in assets. The small fund has the ability to buy any stock it wants without affecting the stock's price. Furthermore, the performance of just a few holdings can have a big bearing on the fund's performance. Another factor favoring managers of small funds is that they are freer to make bets that might pay off big. If the bets fail, the fund does not have much to lose. If the bets pay off and the fund performs well, assets pour in and the fund's management fees skyrocket.

On the other hand, a $5 billion asset base is just too big to buy many small-capitalization stocks, since the fund's buying appetite would drive the share price higher. A big fund may have trouble liquidating shares in a small company if it owns a disproportionate amount of the company's stock. Also, a big fund has less incentive to strive for superior performance, since the fund's management fees (which are based on total assets in the fund), whether or not the fund does well, are huge. Thus, the tendency exists for big funds to follow the status quo and not make big bets in order to enhance performance. The upshot is that as a fund's assets grow, the path to mediocrity shortens.

A good example of the problems facing a big mutual fund was seen in the Fidelity Magellan Fund (assets of more than $50 billion) when it was run by Jeffrey Vinik. The size of Magellan made it difficult to buy the types of stocks Vinik wanted to buy at a given point in time. Think about it for a minute. Even if the fund holds 500 stocks, the average investment in each stock is a whopping $100 million. Many small-cap stocks don't even have market capitalizations of $100 million (market capitalization is the number of outstanding shares multiplied by the stock price). The size of Magellan means that the universe of stocks it can buy is greatly reduced. Anytime you hamstring the investment process by eliminating stocks, you hurt the fund's potential performance. Now, what usually happens is that the fund relegates itself to mediocre performance, since there's no benefit to try for big gains. After all, management fees on the Fidelity Magellan Fund amount to hundreds of millions of dollars per year, even if the fund doesn't receive another dollar in assets or post any gains for shareholders.

There's no real incentive for anyone to try to do great things with a fund that size. That didn't stop Vinik, who tried to better the fund's performance by employing that dreaded of all tools—market timing. Vinik decided to make a big bet on bonds. The result? He was not fully invested in stocks during a time when the stock market was rising, and performance of the fund suffered. What did Vinik get for his efforts to generate market-beating returns? Although reports are a bit unclear as to who initiated the action, Vinik is no longer at Fidelity.

REMEMBER: *There's little incentive to be a hero when you're managing a big fund, which usually translates into, at best, average performance for the fund.*

All this leads me to what I think is the best way to pick a mutual fund. Find a fund family with depth of research and a track record of strong returns across various equity funds. (I like Fidelity—800-544-8888—and Neuberger & Berman—800-877-9700—as starting points.) Look at the fund choices among these fund families, focusing on general equity funds. Choose the general equity fund that has the least amount of assets.

Why do I like this strategy? Several reasons. The small size gives the fund manager a lot of flexibility in terms of what stocks to purchase. The fund manager has every incentive to do well, since strong performance draws money. A small fund within a big and successful fund family can leverage off that fund family's research department. Finally, since competition to run a fund at most big fund families is keen, the fund family usually doesn't accept mediocre results for long.

PRINCIPAL-AGENT ISSUES

Is your fund manager acting in your best interests?

Not much has been said about the downside of giving control of your funds to a fund manager. While transferring responsibility for your money to a fund manager may be prudent in certain instances, it's not without its costs.

First, most mutual funds underperform the market. And with the number of mutual funds growing, the real talent in the field will continue to be spread thinner and thinner.

Second, mutual funds cost money in the way of load fees, redemption fees, 12b-1 marketing fees, and annual management and administrative fees.

Third, when you abdicate responsibility for your investments to a mutual fund, you incur typical principal-agent problems. For example, do you know what your fund manager is doing? And in whose best interest is the manager doing it?

Keep these things in mind the next time you send a check to your favorite mutual fund.

BANKS AND MUTUAL FUNDS

Mutual funds sold by banks are not federally insured.

Many banks across the country now offer their customers mutual funds. Before you invest in a mutual fund offered by your bank, you need to know a few things about the safety of those funds.

First, mutual funds go up and down in value, regardless of whether they are sold by your bank or by your broker. Most people believe that money invested with a bank will not lose value. However, mutual funds offered by the bank are vulnerable to the same market forces that affect other mutual funds.

BOTTOM LINE: *Investing in mutual funds, whether at your bank or through your broker, carries risks.*

Second, investments in mutual funds at the bank are not federally insured. While your savings or checking accounts may be guaranteed by the Federal Deposit Insurance Corp., your investment in a bank's mutual fund is not.

Third, mutual funds charge fees. Just because the fund is offered by the bank does not necessarily mean that you won't have to pay certain fees to invest.

Whenever you invest in a mutual fund offered by your bank, make sure you are aware of the risks, and always make sure to read the fund prospectus before investing.

FUND "FRONT RUNNING"

Front running occurs when fund managers buy shares for their own account and then buy the shares for the fund.

Few industries have maintained such a squeaky-clean image as the mutual-fund industry. The fact that there haven't been any major scandals in the industry is probably one reason for the huge popularity of mutual funds over the last decade.

Periodically, however, the industry's clean image becomes a bit tarnished by concerns over "front running," potentially at the expense of fundholders. Front running occurs when fund managers buy stocks for their own accounts and then buy the shares for the fund. Managers who know they will eventually buy large chunks of stock—thus driving up the price—make a nice profit on shares they buy for their own account ahead of time.

How widespread front running is in the industry is not known. However, when you consider the literally thousands of mutual funds that compete for your money, chances are the practice occurs more often than you'd like to think.

At this point, the problem doesn't appear to have caused any permanent damage, and the mutual-fund industry has swiftly moved to strengthen trading compliance rules. Still, with trillions of dollars now invested in mutual funds, the stakes have risen dramatically for illicit behavior to occur.

REVOLVING DOORS

What should you do when the fund changes managers?

The shake-up in fund managers at Fidelity Investments over the last year brings up an interesting point: When should you bail out of a fund if its manager changes?

I'm not sure there is a right or wrong answer to this question. However, when sizing up a change in fund management, consider these factors:

- *What was the new fund manager's record at his or her previous fund?* If the fund manager achieved success at one fund, it's possible that the success could carry over to the new fund. Keep in mind that having success with a fund of $100 million in assets doesn't necessarily mean that the fund manager will be able to use the same investment strategies with a fund of $10 billion in assets. As a rule, the greater the fund's assets, the more difficult to manage for market-beating performance.

- *What is the depth of expertise at the fund group?* A large fund group, such as Fidelity, has an excellent "minor league" system for training future fund managers. A much smaller fund group may not have the depth of expertise and experience. A shift in fund managers at a smaller fund group should be looked at more closely.

- *Why did the change in fund managers occur?* If the popular fund manager found a better offer and moved to a new firm, it could be that the new manager was chosen in haste. On the other hand, a shift in fund managers precipitated by the fund group probably means that the chain of succession was well thought out in advance, and the right person probably has been selected to run the fund.

FUND MERGERS

You can expect to see more mutual funds merge over the next several years.

I t's estimated that approximately 75 percent of mutual-fund assets are controlled by just 30 mutual-fund companies, according to industry sources. And more mergers in the industry are likely.

Which brings us to an interesting point. What do you do if your mutual fund is acquired? Obviously, it's important to evaluate the track record of the new fund family. This information should be available from the new owners of the mutual fund. Also, examine any management fees and expenses implemented by the new owners. Are fees increasing? Have redemption fees been implemented?

Finally, it pays to examine the breadth of alternatives within the mutual-fund family to make sure that the group's variety of mutual funds meets your needs.

INDEX FUNDS

Index mutual funds mimic a certain index, such as the S&P 500.

The mutual-fund industry is one in which mediocrity is well rewarded. Even though more than two-thirds of actively managed equity funds fail to match market returns in a given year, money continues to pour into these funds. Why? The industry has done a masterful job at selling the benefits of funds—diversification, professional management, ease of investing—while glossing over the fact that performance of most mutual funds is, at best, average.

The fact that beating the market, or even matching market returns, is the exception among funds means that investors should earmark some of their fund investments for index mutual funds.

What are index mutual funds? These are funds which mimic a certain index, such as the Standard & Poor's 500.

The benefits of index funds are many. Investors in these funds are assured of roughly matching the performance of the index. Investing in an S&P 500 index fund means that you'll likely outperform as many as three-quarters of all diversified equity mutual funds over the course of a given year. Because no active management is required to run an index fund—the fund manager simply buys the stocks in the index and weights them accordingly—expenses in these funds are much lower than the expenses of actively managed funds. Lower expenses mean that more of your money is working for you.

The Vanguard fund family (800-662-7447) offers a variety of funds mimicking a number of indexes. Contact Vanguard for further information.

INDEX INVESTING–WITH A TWIST

The Vanguard Growth & Income Fund offers investors a way to have their cake and eat it too.

If you buy the notion that owning an index fund makes sense, but you still want the possibility of beating the market, consider what I call "near" index funds.

A near index fund structures its portfolio similarly to an index fund but tweaks the portfolio just a bit in order to attempt to outperform the index.

My favorite fund in this category is the Vanguard Growth & Income Fund, formerly the Vanguard Quantitative Index Fund (800-662-7447). This no-load fund contains many of the same securities as are in the Standard & Poor's 500 index. However, instead of duplicating the exact weighting of the investments as they are found in the S&P 500, the Growth & Income Fund, using various fundamental stock-picking tools, gives different weightings to the stocks depending on how the stocks fare under the fund manager's valuation model. The hope is that by assuming a "quasi" index look, but still having active management, the fund can outperform the index or, in the worst case, not stray too far on the downside.

Now some of you are probably saying that applying any human touch to a fund makes a fund no index fund at all, and I agree. Still, I think this "near index" fund is an excellent alternative for investors who want to take a middle-of-the-road approach between an index and actively managed fund.

How has the fund done in recent years? Very well. In fact, the fund has outperformed Vanguard's own Index Trust 500 Fund (a pure index fund) over the last 10 years.

BOND FUNDS

Just because a bond fund advertises itself as "guaranteed" doesn't mean you can't have losses.

A re all bond funds alike?
The answer is a resounding no.

There are a number of factors investors should consider before investing in bond funds.

Bond prices move in the opposite direction of interest rates. When interest rates rise, bond values fall. Investors can shield themselves from the volatility of interest-rate movements by buying short-term bond funds. These funds will be much less volatile than long-term bonds during interest-rate movements. In addition, it is important to consider the quality of the bonds in the portfolio.

Finally, investors should be aware that because the fund advertises itself as "guaranteed" does not mean that investors are guaranteed against loss of principal. The guarantee usually refers only to interest payments.

For maximum safety, it is best to stay with short- to intermediate-term bond funds that invest in only the highest-quality bonds. Also, since there has never been any conclusive evidence linking sales charges for mutual funds to superior performance, bond fund investors should focus on no-load bond funds.

MUTUAL-FUND YIELDS

Funds must follow standardized rules for determining and advertising fund yields.

Mutual-fund yields, particularly yields on income funds, have been a source of confusion for investors. However, the Securities and Exchange Commission has taken steps in recent years to remedy the situation.

Mutual funds now have to follow standardized rules for determining and advertising mutual-fund yields. The rules require a standard formula for calculating advertised yields on bond funds. The SEC took the measures because of what it perceived to be misleading yields in some instances.

The new rules bring up an interesting point: How much should investors rely on advertised yields in choosing a mutual fund? Of course, it pays to factor in the yield when the emphasis is on income. However, there are other considerations. Does the fund have a load fee? It does not pay to purchase a load bond fund, since the quality and risk levels of assets in the fund may differ little from those in a no-load bond fund.

Finally, investors should consider the interest-rate climate. A high-yielding fund generally holds investments with long-term maturities and thus will be more vulnerable to a loss of principal should interest rates rise.

GNMA FUNDS

Your investment principal may fluctuate in a Ginnie Mae fund.

GNMA funds, or Ginnie Maes, have become a popular income vehicle for investors. GNMA funds invest in a pool of federally insured mortgage loans and pass through all payments of interest and principal to fundholders. Before investing in Ginnie Maes, it is important to be aware of some factors which can dramatically affect your returns from these investments.

If you invest in a Ginnie Mae fund, the holding should be looked upon as a long-term investment, since interest-rate changes can make the principal of the fund fluctuate dramatically in the short run. Another factor unique to Ginnie Maes is the problem that arises when interest rates fall and prepayments of mortgages rise. Under this scenario, the mortgage payments come more quickly than expected and therefore have to be reinvested, usually at lower rates. It is not unusual for the yields on Ginnie Mae funds to drop during periods of falling interest rates and high mortgage prepayments.

The one mistake that I see concerning Ginnie Maes is that individuals who are desperate for income tend to load up on them. Such poor portfolio diversification often leads to problems when the funds don't perform well because of the prevailing interest-rate environment.

Investors should balance Ginnie Mae holdings in their portfolio with other investments, such as stocks, corporate bonds, CDs, and money markets.

SELLING MUTUAL FUNDS

Switching out of one bond or stock fund into another is a taxable transaction.

Despite their popularity, mutual funds are not readily understood by investors, especially when it comes to selling shares and accounting for the sale for tax purposes.

Many mutual-fund families have made switching funds as easy as making a phone call. However, many investors don't realize that every time they switch mutual funds that are held outside of a retirement account, they are generating a taxable transaction. Switching from one mutual fund to another mutual fund within the same family is the equivalent of selling one stock and buying another. Such transactions usually generate capital gains or losses on which income taxes must be calculated.

Adding to the complexity of the situation is the check-writing privilege that some mutual-fund firms give holders. Writing a check against holdings in a money-market account does not constitute a taxable transaction. However, many bond funds permit investors to write checks against their accounts. For investors who take advantage of this feature, every time they write a check against their bond fund to pay the mortgage or buy a gift, it constitutes a sale of the fund and creates a potential tax liability for the investor.

BOTTOM LINE: *Know the rules when selling fund shares to avoid any tax surprises.*

DETERMINING THE COST BASIS OF FUND SHARES

Some of the bigger mutual-fund families provide average-cost calculations.

If you've ever sold a chunk of your mutual fund, you know the potential problems that come at tax time when you have to determine the cost basis on the shares sold.

Fortunately, some mutual funds bring relief to clients at tax time by providing assistance on determining cost basis. Mutual-fund investors can use one of four methods to determine the cost basis on fund shares they sell:

- First in, first out, in which the first shares bought are considered the first shares sold

- Identified cost, in which shareholders must identify which shares they have sold

- Average-basis single category, in which the costs of all shares in the fund account are averaged

- Average-basis double category, in which the average-cost method is used, except that long-term and short-term holdings are averaged in separate categories

Some of the bigger mutual-fund families provide average-cost calculations. If you are faced with some difficulties in determining your cost on fund shares that you sell, the first place to go for help is the fund family's customer service.

INTERNATIONAL MUTUAL FUNDS

International funds provide an easy way to diversify a portfolio overseas.

Given that international mutual funds have not been great performers in recent years, many investors have turned their backs on this area. However, investors' cold shoulders are precisely why these funds deserve a second look.

Granted, the international arena has traditionally been

much more volatile. However, international investing does provide a boost to portfolio diversification. In addition, growth potential in some international economies is far greater than that of the U.S. economy, and that should translate into strong stock performances abroad over time.

From an asset allocation standpoint, investors with reasonably long time horizons—15 to 20 years until retirement—ought to have a healthy percentage of their holdings in international investments, perhaps 15 percent to 20 percent.

If you believe you are underrepresented in the international sector, now is the time to beef up holdings given the depressed prices of many international mutual funds. Two no-load funds which provide high-quality ways to play the international sector are the T. Rowe Price International Stock Fund (800-638-5660) and Acorn International Fund (800-922-6769).

DIVERSIFYING A PORTFOLIO OF MUTUAL FUNDS

You can have adequate diversification with a portfolio of just five or six funds.

Diversification is a term most often used with stocks. For example, "How many stocks should you own in a portfolio to achieve decent diversification?" (The answer is 13 to 17.) You can also apply diversification principles to your mutual-fund holdings. How many funds are the right amount to hold to be properly diversified?

Interestingly, a "portfolio" of mutual funds almost seems redundant. After all, one mutual fund could hold 200 to 300 individual stocks. Thus, diversifying among mutual funds can be a tricky proposition. For example, owning three general equity funds may give you "fund manager" diversification, but such funds probably invest in the same types of stocks. The correlation of the funds' performances can be expected to be fairly similar.

When diversifying among funds, you should focus on types of investments, not necessarily on the hottest funds. For example, you might want to construct a portfolio consisting of the following no-load funds:

- *One index fund.* An index fund mimics the performance of a popular market index, such as the Standard & Poor's 500. I suggest indexing the S&P 500 with the Vanguard Index Trust 500 Fund (800-662-7447).

- *One fund devoted to small-capitalization stocks.* In this category, I like the Vanguard Index Small-Cap Stock Fund (800-662-7447). I also consider the Strong Schafer Value Fund (800-368-1030) an excellent choice for a general equity fund.

- *One bond fund.* In this category, I like the Vanguard Bond Index Total Bond Market Fund (800-662-7447), an index fund for bonds.

- *One fund devoted to international stocks.* Two top-quality selections in this group are T. Rowe Price International Stock Fund (800-638-5660) and Acorn International Fund (800-922-6769).

Once you've made your fund selections, the second step is proper allocation of funds. Obviously, how much money you put into stock funds will depend on your age, income level, risk aversion, and so on. As a rule, take 110 minus your age as a reasonable amount to devote to equity funds. The remainder should be in bond funds and cash.

CLOSED-END FUNDS

Closed-end funds often trade at discounts to the value of the funds' assets.

C losed-end funds are similar to open-end funds in that the funds permit investment in a basket of stocks selected and managed by an investment company. However, there are a few major differences. Open-end funds continually sell new shares to the public and redeem shares at the fund's net asset value— the market value of the firm's portfolio of stocks minus short-term liabilities. Closed-end funds, however, sell only a certain number of shares at the initial public offering, just as with a stock. Once the shares are sold, the fund is "closed," and new money is not accepted.

Another major difference is that closed-end funds trade on the stock exchanges, while open-end funds do not. Because closed-end funds are publicly traded, their prices are set by supply and demand among various investors, just as with common stocks. Thus, unlike open-end funds, which always redeem shares at the net asset value, closed-end funds often trade above or below their net asset value, and sometimes these premiums or discounts are quite large. How do you know if a closed-end fund is trading at a discount or premium? Such information is given periodically in *The Wall Street Journal* and in every issue of *Barron's*.

Here are some factors to consider when investing in a closed-end fund:

- Merely because a closed-end fund is trading at a discount doesn't make it a good investment. Evaluate if the fund meets your investment objective and fits in with the rest of your portfolio.

- Keep a close eye on fund expenses. One rule of thumb is never invest in a closed-end fund unless its discount is roughly 10 times its annual expense ratio.

- Avoid investing in closed-end funds that trade at a premium to their net asset values.

Discounts on closed-end funds appear to have widened this year. One explanation for the current spate of discounts is that investors, in their desire to throw money at the thousands of open-end mutual funds—many of which can be bought directly from the mutual-fund family, without a broker—are simply ignoring the opportunities in closed-end funds, thus allowing the discounts to persist.

History has shown that the time to buy closed-end funds—as is the case with any investment—is when they are out of favor. Once investors return to closed-end funds, the discounts shrink quickly.

CLOSED-END FUND IPOs

Never buy a closed-end fund at its initial public offering.

If your broker calls you with the latest hot tip concerning a closed-end fund's initial public offering (IPO), tell the broker to call you back in about six months.

In a three-year study by the SEC's Office of Economic Analysis, closed-end funds were shown, on average, to be a bad deal when purchased at the initial public offering. That's because soon after the offering, most closed-end funds dropped sharply in price.

The study showed that closed-end funds plunged an average of 15.1 percent during the first 120 trading days, after the overall market return is subtracted. This price drop reflects, in part, the money that goes to pay the underwriters who brought the fund public. Investors who would like to add a closed-end fund to their portfolios would be better off waiting three to six months after the fund goes public before making purchases.

FOLLOW THE FUND MANAGER

When a fund closes its doors, see if another fund in the family is managed by the same manager.

With billions of dollars flowing into mutual funds, many hot fund managers are closing their funds' doors. That's because too much money makes their jobs more difficult, and fund returns suffer.

There may still be a way to have a hot fund manager manage your money. In big fund families, it is not uncommon for an individual to manage more than one mutual fund. It is quite possible that, even though a fund closes its doors to new money, another fund in the group, with the same manager, may be accepting money. Check with the fund family if you want to invest with a particular fund manager.

Another approach is to see if the fund manager also manages a closed-end fund. Some fund managers manage both open-end and closed-end funds with the same investment objectives. It may be the case that the closed-end fund is selling at a discount to net asset value, which means you buy the fund manager's expertise more cheaply via the closed-end fund than through the open-end mutual fund.

8

RETIREMENT INVESTING

Nearly twice as many young adults believe in the existence of E.T. than in the likelihood of ever cashing a social security check.

According to *Smart Money* magazine, a survey of young adults showed that 46 percent believe in extraterrestrial life. Only 28 percent believe that social security will exist when they retire.

That the long-term solvency of social security ranks well below space aliens on young adults' believability scale may be hard to fathom for individuals currently cashing social security checks. Trust me—the fears of the eventual extinction of social security are quite real, and not just with adults in their twenties and thirties. Plenty of baby boomers in their forties and fifties have little faith that social security will be there for them either.

Some experts believe these fears are unfounded. With adjustments to the system—allowing social security funds to be invested in mutual funds seems to be a favorite fix for some pundits—social security will be around for a very long time to meet the needs of tomorrow's retirees.

Let's assume that these experts are right. Does that mean that tomorrow's retirees can rest easy, relying exclusively on social security as a means to enjoy those golden years? It's important to understand that few people currently receiving social security checks live the life of Riley. The percentage of retirees who rely on social security for half or more of their income is 66 percent; the percentage of elderly who would fall below the poverty line without social security benefits is 54 percent.

Regardless of whether social security will be around when you get the gold watch, it's clear that you will have an increasing responsibility for your financial well-being during retirement. The government, by liberalizing certain rules regarding retirement investing, has been telling you this for years.

For example, a new tax law that began in 1997 allows nonworking spouses to invest up to $2,000 annually in an Individual Retirement Account, up from the previous $250 limit. Is the government allowing your family to shield more money in tax-preferenced IRAs because it loves to lose tax revenues? Of course not. Each time Uncle Sam liberalizes rules surrounding retirement investing, he is saying, "I'm helping you help yourself; don't expect my help down the road, because my pockets may be empty."

What can you do to ensure a financially sound retirement? Obviously, the sooner you get started investing for retirement, the better. Also, avoid the common mistake of being too conservative with your money. If you have 20 years or more to retirement, the bulk of your retirement funds should be invested in stocks, either directly or through a mutual fund.

Of course, if the 46 percent of young adults who believe in extraterrestrial life are right, the solution to the social security problem is a no-brainer:

Make E.T. pay FICA.

Ah, if it were only that easy.

CAN YOU AFFORD RETIREMENT?

You'll need 70 percent to 80 percent of your final working income to maintain a similar lifestyle in retirement.

In a survey conducted by Fidelity Investments and Yankelovich & Partners, the majority of participants cited retirement as their top reason for saving. And yet the same survey stated that among respondents age 40 and over, more than one-third have saved less than $30,000 toward retirement.

There really is no secret to investing for retirement. The key is just getting started, and the earlier the better. For example, a 22-year-old who invests just $500 each year (or about $1.37 per day) until age 62, assuming that money earns an average annual return of 10 percent, will have a nest egg of nearly one quarter of a million dollars.

Remember it's estimated that you'll need 70 percent to 80 percent of your final working income to maintain a similar lifestyle in retirement.

Now, can you still afford retirement?

401(K) PLANS

Contributions to a 401(k) not only help feather your nest egg but also reduce your yearly tax bite.

Perhaps the most effective avenue for saving for your retirement is a 401(k), yet many investors miss out on this excellent investment opportunity.

Briefly, 401(k) plans, which are offered by many companies, are basically self-imposed savings plans, with agreed-upon amounts of money taken directly from each paycheck. As with typical retirement plans, 401(k) contributions build tax-deferred over time.

But a 401(k) plan has several kickers that enhance its attractiveness. Whereas the upper limit in IRA contributions is $2,000 annually, you can contribute more to a 401(k). And you can contribute to a 401(k) plan even if you already have an IRA.

Perhaps best of all, contributions to a 401(k) are made with pretax dollars. In other words, although you pay social security and Medicare taxes on your contributions, these amounts are not included on your W-2 form as taxable wages or income. Thus, contributions to a 401(k) not only help to feather your nest egg but also reduce your yearly tax bite.

There are usually penalties associated with withdrawal of 401(k) money before age $59\frac{1}{2}$, so consult a tax adviser before dipping into these funds. For further information about the 401(k) plan where you work, consult with your employer. It is possible that your employer matches part of your contribution to a 401(k) plan.

SAVE FOR RETIREMENT WITH PRETAX DOLLARS

The beauty of a 401(k) plan is that you save for retirement with pretax dollars.

There is no better way to save for retirement than with pretax dollars that accumulate tax-deferred. That's the beauty of a 401(k) plan.

For example, let's say you invest $300 per month in your company's 401(k) plan. Assuming you are in the 28 percent tax bracket, you would have to pay a little more than $1,000 in taxes on these earnings if you did not contribute the money to the 401(k) plan. In other words, your $3,600 investment in the 401(k) is really costing you only about $2,600 when you account for the tax savings.

Another way to look at a 401(k) plan is the following: If you wanted to make a $3,600 investment outside of a 401(k) plan, you would have to earn $5,000 in order to net a $3,600 investment after taxes (assuming a 28 percent tax bracket).

Keep in mind that many employers match a portion of your investment in a 401(k) plan. And remember—the earnings on investments in your 401(k) plan are growing tax-deferred.

BOTTOM LINE: If a 401(k) is available to you, do whatever you can to invest in it, even if it is a nominal amount each paycheck. In fact, in most cases, it is foolish to invest in other retirement vehicles until you have maxed out your 401(k) investments. The maximum pretax contribution an employee can make to a 401(k) plan in 1997 is $9,500.

THE SEDUCTION OF EMPLOYER 401(K) "MATCHING"

Limit your company's stock in your 401(k) plan to 25 percent or less.

One of the benefits of many 401(k) retirement plans is that your employer will match some percentage of the amount you invest. What could be better than free money, right?

The problem is that not all matching plans are the same. For example, many companies offer company stock as a matching contribution. Owning company stock is not necessarily a bad thing. In fact, having your interest aligned with company shareholders by being a stockholder is good—to a point. The problem arises when you have too much of a good thing.

Rogers Casey & Associates, a pension consulting firm, surveyed 500 companies about their 401(k) plans. What it found was rather interesting:

- About 42 percent of the assets in large-company plans are invested in the employers' stock.

- Some 34 percent of the employers surveyed are "somewhat concerned" with the level of employee assets invested in the company; 11 percent are "very concerned."

Of course, if your company's stock is rising at an above-average rate, so is the value of your pension plan. But what happens when the stock market turns south? Or worse, when your company's stock hits an air pocket, taking with it your retirement nest egg?

Employer matching plans with company stock can be quite seductive. After all, who wouldn't want to buy stock 50 cents or 75 cents on the dollar? Such discounts on company stock are common in 401(k) plans. Don't be seduced. Follow prudent portfolio diversification strategies when building your 401(k) plan. Try to limit your company's stock in your plan to 25 percent or less.

REMEMBER: *You already have a lot at stake with your company by virtue of having a job with the firm. Don't get killed twice—losing your job and your retirement funds—in the event the firm goes belly up.*

To check out how your pension funds are allocated across investments, contact the plan trustee where you work.

403(B) PLANS

403(b) plans are similar to 401(k) plans.

If you work for a nonprofit organization, such as a school, university, hospital, or research institute, chances are you are eligible to invest in a 403(b) plan.

A 403(b) plan works much the same way as a 401(k) plan. Contributions to the plan come "right off the top" and lower your taxable income for income tax purposes. The maximum annual contribution to a 403(b) plan at the time of this writing is $9,500.

A simple example shows the power of investing in a 403(b) plan. Let's say you are the head of the United Way and make $25 million per year. (Some of those nonprofit guys make big dough—really big dough as was discovered at the United Way.) Anyway, you make $25 million per year. If you invest the maximum $9,500 in your 403(b) fund, you'll lower your taxable income by a like amount. If you're in the 39 percent tax bracket, that means you've trimmed your taxes by more than $3,700 by investing the maximum in your 403(b).

If you are eligible for a 403(b) plan where your work, you should max out your investments in the plan first before you put your money into any other retirement vehicles.

THE DANGER OF RISK AVOIDANCE

Purging a portfolio of risk means relegating your portfolio to mediocre returns.

Few things are more harmful to retirement savings than risk avoidance.

On the surface, this sounds like a silly statement. Avoiding risk is a good thing, right? Unfortunately, purging a portfolio of risk means relegating your portfolio to returns that are inadequate for building and sustaining a retirement nest egg.

I come across a lot of individuals who, when hitting the age of retirement, believe that they must "batten down the hatches" and avoid taking any risk with their investments. All their money goes into a money-market fund, a certificate of deposit, or perhaps a short-term bond fund. Even worse, I can't tell you how many times I've seen individuals in their twenties and thirties—even individuals in my own company—set up 401(k) plans void of stocks in an effort to avoid risk.

Several problems exist with such a conservative approach. First, just because you've retired doesn't mean that your investment horizon is zero. Many people live well into their eighties and beyond—20 to 30 years after they retire. With such a long life span following retirement, it is important to have growth components in your retirement portfolio, if for no other reason than to keep pace with inflation.

Thus, I don't think it's being too aggressive for a 70-year-old to have 30 percent of a retirement account in stocks or equity mutual funds. And for a worker in his or her twenties or thirties, a 401(k) plan should contain almost exclusively equity funds.

TRADING YOUR 401(K) PLAN

The best approach for a 401(k) plan is to pick an asset allocation that makes sense and stick with it.

It's been shown that trying to time the market is a loser's game. Sure, you're going to get lucky every now and again. However, timing will more than likely prove hazardous to your wealth. Despite the mounds of evidence in favor of buy-and-hold investing, many investors still trade in and out of the market. Worse, they trade with retirement money.

The advent of 401(k) plans has made all of us money managers, whether we like it or not. And while it may seem like a benefit to be able to shift money in our 401(k) at a moment's notice, what this "flexibility" has done is turned a lot of us into traders. Unfortunately, just about the time you move money out of stocks and into bonds, it's probably the time you should be buying stocks, not selling.

The best strategy for a 401(k) plan is to pick an asset allocation that makes sense for your age, income level, and investment time horizon. Once you've determined your asset allocation, buy the appropriate mutual funds on the basis of this allocation. Lastly, don't get caught up moving money in and out of funds. Be patient and do as little trading as possible.

PENSION ROLLOVER

Have your old employer roll over a pension directly into your new account.

When you are rolling over a pension account, it's critical to be aware of some key points.

Investors have 60 days in which to perform their pension rollover if they take possession of funds from a previous employer. However, individuals who take possession of pension funds rather than having them transferred directly from their previous employer to a qualified plan may be in for a surprise.

If funds are distributed to you, 20 percent of the amount will be withheld for income taxes. In order to roll the whole amount into an IRA, you have to make up the 20 percent. If you do this, you'll get the 20 percent back when you file your tax return.

In most cases, if you do not invest the entire amount, including the 20 percent that is withheld, you will be taxed on that 20 percent as ordinary income plus be liable for a penalty if you are under the age of $59^1/_2$. Have your former employer send the payment directly to the administrator of your new plan, and consult your tax adviser.

IRA INVESTING

The argument for investing in an IRA, even if your contributions aren't tax-deductible, is compelling.

Tax-law changes a number of years ago scared off many investors from contributing to an Individual Retirement Account. However, the main benefit of an IRA—the accumulation of tax-deferred income for retirement—remains intact.

The tax-law changes over the years concerning IRAs primarily affected deductibility of contributions. Deductions for contributions are eliminated if the adjusted gross income is more than $50,000 for joint filers or $35,000 for single filers who are covered by employers' pension plans. For incomes from $40,000 to $50,000 for joint filers and $25,000 to $35,000 for a single return, deductions are reduced on a sliding scale, with a minimum deduction of $200. Filers under these income levels retain full deductibility.

The argument for investing in an IRA is still compelling. Assume an investor contributes $2,000 annually over a 25-year period to an IRA and achieves an annual growth rate of 10 percent. The fund will accumulate to $216,000, or roughly 38 percent more than a fund earning the same return but on which annual taxes are paid.

For IRA investments, I believe it is important to include stocks with decent yields and dividend growth prospects. Such investments allow you to take advantage of the magic of compounding that occurs in a long-term investment account such as an IRA.

IRAs AND "NONWORKING SPOUSES"

Nonworking spouses are now on level ground with working spouses in terms of IRA contributions.

If you are what the tax code refers to as a "nonworking spouse," you've probably felt like a second-class citizen when it comes to investing in an Individual Retirement Account (IRA).

Even though you may be at home slugging it out with repair people, kids, pets, and other sources of domestic insurrections, the tax code in years past deemed that your efforts were worth a maximum contribution of only $250 per year in an IRA. Your "working" husband or wife, on the other hand, could contribute up to $2,000 annually.

Fortunately, beginning in 1997, "nonworking spouses" are now on level ground with working spouses in terms of IRA contributions. The rule change now permits working and nonworking spouses to contribute up to a maximum of $2,000 per year in an IRA. This amount can be contributed whether the working spouse is covered by a qualified pension plan or not.

The benefits to investing in an IRA are twofold: (1) earnings in an IRA are tax-deferred; and (2) depending on family income levels and the availability of an employer-sponsored retirement plan, contributions to an IRA may be tax deductible.

If you and your spouse have the financial wherewithal, take advantage of the $2,000 contribution limit for non-working spouses. A good place to put such IRA money is in the Vanguard Wellesley Income Fund (800-662-7447). This no-load fund consists of approximately one-third stocks and two-thirds bonds and has an excellent performance record, especially when adjusted for risk. Helping the fund's performance are low annual management fees.

 # LUMP-SUM INVESTING

A study shows that investing a lump sum is better than dollar-cost averaging.

To invest a lump sum or to space out investments over time is the question facing many individuals these days. Interestingly, a study indicates that investors are better off investing the lump sum.

Richard Williams and Peter Bacon of Wright State University, in a detailed study covering the years 1926 to 1991, suggest that nearly two-thirds of the time, a lump-sum strategy significantly outperformed a dollar-cost averaging strategy. One reason is that the stock market historically has risen more often than it has declined. Thus, holding money on the sidelines generally costs investors in lost returns.

Does this refute dollar-cost averaging? Certainly not. Keep in mind that what we are talking about is a lump-sum investment. Dollar-cost averaging is best exploited when an investment program is geared over the long term and when monthly installments are made, usually because large amounts of cash aren't available in a lump sum to invest. Also, while expected returns from lump-sum investing may be higher, risks may be greater as well relative to dollar-cost averaging.

TAXES AND RETIREMENT INVESTING

One mistake investors make is to ignore the role of taxes in shaping retirement investing strategies.

When building a retirement account, keep in mind how taxes affect your investments:

- For many people, especially those in the highest tax brackets, dividends and interest income in investments held outside a retirement account are taxed at higher rates than long-term capital gains.

- You cannot take advantage of losses if you sell an investment in a tax-preferred account.

- When you own individual stocks, you control your tax destiny to a large extent. You incur a tax liability (other than taxes on dividends) only when you sell an investment. You don't have control over your tax destiny with mutual funds. You incur a potential tax liability when the mutual-fund manager decides to make a capital-gains distribution.

Because of the interplay of taxes with your investments, it's not a bad idea to take into account the following rules of thumb when saving for retirement:

- Preference income-generating investments in tax-preferenced accounts. Does this mean that you should never hold stocks in an IRA or a 401(k) plan? Certainly not. However, it does mean that it's not a bad idea to weight your portfolio a bit toward higher-yielding investments—total-return stocks, balanced mutual funds, and so on—in order to maximize the tax benefits. Also, preference mutual funds in tax-preferenced accounts. This is one way to mitigate the effects of unwanted capital-gains distributions.

- Consider holding high-growth investments, such as individual stocks, outside of tax-preferenced accounts. In this way, you limit the tax bite by owning stocks (and being able to defer indefinitely capital-gains taxes), and you have the ability to exploit capital losses that occur.

GUARANTEED INVESTMENT CONTRACTS

The problems with GICs drive home the point that there is no such thing as a guaranteed investment.

C hances are, at least part of your company's pension plan is invested in guaranteed investment contracts

(GICs). GICs are sold by insurance companies. Their popularity stems from the fact that high yields are "guaranteed" by the insurance companies. The hitch is that the only guarantee of the yield or, for that matter, the principal is the backing of the insurance company. If investments in which GIC funds are held decline in value, it's up to the insurance company to make good on the investments.

When the insurance industry was suffering from bad junk bond and real estate investments, weak insurers ran into trouble with their GIC investments. The past problems with GICs of certain insurance companies drive home the point that there is no such thing as a guaranteed investment. All investments have some degree of risk, whether it be market risk, default risk, interest-rate risk, or all three.

In fact, some GICs are now changing their names from guaranteed to such words as "assured interest," according to *The Wall Street Journal*.

What should you do as an investor? Obviously, be aware of how your retirement dollars are being invested by your company.

Ask questions.

Read pension plan prospectuses.

Most important, use prudent diversification practices and don't depend on just one investment to build your nest egg.

TAX-DEFERRED ANNUITIES

Unlike an IRA, an annuity is not restricted to a maximum $2,000 investment per year.

It is quite likely that you've been given the pitch for tax-deferred annuities by your broker or insurance salesperson. It's also quite likely that you have no idea what these investments are.

An annuity is a contract between you and an insurance company in which you pay a set amount of money and, at a stated point, receive a predetermined amount of money, most of the time for life.

The major plus is that the money you pay accumulates tax-deferred, just like the funds in an IRA. In this respect, an annuity is similar to an IRA. Another attractive feature of an annuity is that, unlike an IRA, it is not restricted to a maximum $2,000 per year.

There are two kinds of annuities—fixed and flexible. Fixed annuities are invested in fixed-income investments that guarantee a floor rate of interest. Flexible annuities can consist of bonds, stocks, real estate, and other investments. There are also single-premium annuities, which are purchased with a one-time payment, and installment annuities, which are purchased with periodic payments.

What are some things to consider when purchasing an annuity?

- Annuities can be very expensive. Know how much you are paying in commissions when purchasing an annuity. One mutual-fund family that offers relatively low-priced annuity contracts is Vanguard (800-662-7447).

- Annuities are not guaranteed or under any federal insurance program. It is critical that you invest in annuities of only the strongest issuers. A. M. Best Co. is a rater of annuities, and its rating book can be found in most libraries.

- Check on the penalties of cashing in an annuity before the age of $59\frac{1}{2}$.

- Evaluate the portfolio in which the money is invested. Does the annuity invest in junk bonds, risky stocks, or real estate? Keep in mind that annuities with unusually high yields are probably investments with above-average risk.

- Don't be greedy. If the salesperson trumpets the potentially high return, this could be a red flag that the investment is too risky. There is no free lunch in annuities, and high expected returns on an annuity will carry high risks.

CHECKING UP ON YOUR SOCIAL SECURITY HOLDINGS

You can know exactly the amount in your social security account by contacting the agency.

Have you ever wondered exactly where all that money you pay in FICA taxes goes? Well, that money goes into the fund for social security. Wouldn't it be nice to know just how much money is in your account?

Fortunately, there's a way to check on your social security holdings by contacting the social security office at (800) 772-1213 and getting a Request for Earnings and Benefits Statement. When you get the statement, fill it out and return it to the social security office. Within a couple of months, you should receive a copy of your social security record, including how much you've paid as well as an estimate of future benefits.

When you get this report, make sure it reflects your entire work history. Occasionally, mistakes are made, and you may not be receiving all the credit you deserve. If you find a mistake, notify the social security office in your area to remedy the situation.

THE TRILLION-DOLLAR TRANSFER

Over $6 trillion in assets will likely be accumulated by parents of baby boomers through 2011.

A re you spending your child's inheritance?

Not all of you are, as evidenced by a *Fortune* magazine article. Over $6 trillion in assets will likely be accumulated by parents of baby boomers through 2011, according to the article. Such wealth could be the biggest windfall of all for the baby boomers. The implications of this transfer of wealth are far-reaching.

Many economists have accused baby boomers of overspending and fear that their lack of savings could have repercussions down the road. However, it could be argued that one reason for their large consumer-spending practices—a major engine of economic growth over the last decade—is that many boomers have annuities awaiting them in the form of their parents' estates.

In what form this trillion-dollar transfer takes place has important ramifications for the financial markets. Obviously, a major component of this asset buildup is real estate values. The gravy train in real estate prices for most of the last two decades created major wealth for some individuals.

As real estate is liquidated to settle estates, substantial amounts of money could end up in stocks and bonds, sending stock and bond prices much higher over the next two decades.

INDEX

ABOUT THE AUTHOR

Chuck Carlson is the best-selling author of *Buying Stocks Without a Broker, No-Load Stocks,* and *Free Lunch on Wall Street*, three investment classics from McGraw-Hill. A frequent guest on financial TV and radio shows and often quoted by the print media, Carlson is the editor of *DRIP Investor* and a contributing editor of the influential *Dow Theory Forecasts* newsletter. He is a Chartered Financial Analyst.

DRIP Investor covers all aspects of no-load stocks and dividend reinvestment plans (DRIPs) — how to buy stocks without a broker, how to buy stocks at a discount, even blue-chips on the "installment plan" for as little as $10 a month.

This authoritative monthly service is written by Charles Carlson, CFA, best-selling author of *No-Load Stocks, Free Lunch on Wall Street, Chuck Carlson's 60 Second Investor*, and *Buying Stocks Without A Broker*. As a *60 Second Investor* reader, you are entitled to receive the Charter Rate of only $59 for a full year — a 25% savings.

With your subscription you will receive a *DRIP Investor* custom 3-ring storage binder plus <u>FREE 32-page DRIP Starter Kit, a step-by-step blueprint to success in no-load stocks and DRIPs</u>. <u>Money-back guarantee.</u> You may cancel any time for a pro rata refund.

To take advantage of this generous offer, tear out this page and mail today . . . **or call toll-free — 1-800-233-5922.**

- - - CHARTER RATE - - -

❑ **YES**, start my subscription to *DRIP Investor* immediately at the Charter Rate of only $59 for one year, a $20 savings. Send FREE storage binder and 32-page DRIP Starter Kit. I may cancel any time for a pro rata refund.

Name   (Please Print)

Address

City   State   Zip

Payment Method ❑ Check or money order

Please charge: ❑ VISA ❑ MasterCard ❑ Discover ❑ American Express

---

Credit Card Number

Expiration Date   Signature required for credit card orders   60I-97

Not valid until accepted by
DRIP *Investor* • **7412 Calumet Ave., Ste. 200** • **Hammond, IN 46324-2692**

Nothing Succeeds Like Success

One prominent observer of stock market advisory services has stated that **"Longevity is the visible evidence of success in the investment newsletter business** because the public will not pay very long for bad advice."

Is it any wonder then that *Dow Theory Forecasts* is so proud of an over **50-year record** of performance . . . serving the needs of individual investors with stock market guidance since 1946.

Dow Theory Forecasts has obviously stood the test of time. This is no "flash in the pan," "johnny-come-lately" investment service. Dozens of competitors of that stripe spring up during bull markets only to disappear after a serious bear market or two.

The loyal support of thousands of regular readers through good markets and bad for over 50 years allows us to continue to offer a high quality service at low cost for the individual investor.

See Special Offer Coupon on back

The author of *Chuck Carlson's 60 Second Investor* invites you to try *Dow Theory Forecasts*